Eyes on Nature®

Animal Kingdom

Copyright © 2000
Kidsbooks, Inc.
3535 West Peterson Ave.
Chicago, IL 60659

All rights reserved including the right of reproduction
in whole or in part in any form.

Manufactured in China
04001D

Visit us at www.kidsbooks.com
Volume discounts available for group purchases.

Table of Contents

MAMMALS..7
    By Rebecca L. Grambo

INSECTS..29
    By John Grassy

REPTILES AND AMPHIBIANS......................................55
    By Robert Matero and Rebecca L. Grambo

BIRDS OF PREY...81
    By Rebecca L. Grambo

Index..106

Glossary..108

Photo Credits: Mammals

Tom Bledsoe: page 13
François Gohier: pages 14, 18-19, 21
Glen & Rebecca L. Grambo: pages 8, 11, 12, 20, 27
Larry Kimball: page 12
Dwight Kuhn: pages 14, 15, 21
Tom & Pat Leeson: pages 16, 20, 22
Kevin Schafer: pages 9, 10, 11, 14, 19, 24, 24-25
Kevin Schafer & Martha Hill: page 17
Marty Snyderman: page 26
Merlin Tuttle: page 21
Art Wolfe: pages 11, 20, 22
Norbert Wu: pages 16, 25
Gavriel Jecan/Art Wolfe Inc.: page 18
Tom Brakefield/DRK: pages 12, 18
J. Cancalosi/DRK: page 12
John Gerlach/DRK: page 8
Johnny Johnson/DRK: page 15
Steven Kaufman/DRK: page 10
Stephen J. Krasemann/DRK: page 22
Ford Kristo/DRK: page 24
Tom & Pat Leeson/DRK: pages 9, 13, 15, 23
Wayne Lynch/DRK: page 23
Joe McDonald/DRK: page 8
Peter Pickford/DRK: page 25
David Woodfall/DRK: page 10
Belinda Wright/DRK: page 21
Gerry Ellis: ENP Images: pages 13, 15, 17, 24, 26
Peter Howorth/Mo Yung Productions: page 9
John D. Cunningham/Visuals Unlimited: pages 22-23
David B. Fleetham/Visuals Unlimited: page 16
Rod Kieft/Visuals Unlimited: page 17
Ken Lucas/Visuals Unlimited: page 18
Joe McDonald/Visuals Unlimited: page 13
R. A. Simpson/Visuals Unlimited: page 19
Gary Walter/Visuals Unlimited: page 23
Stephen Frink/Waterhouse: page 17
Tom DiMauro/Wildlife Collection: page 25
Michael Francis/Wildlife Collection: page 22
D. Robert Franz/Wildlife Collection: page 27
Martin Harvey/ Wildlife Collection: pages 8, 24, 27

Cover Photo Credits:

Gerald & Buff Corsi
Robert & Linda Mitchell
Lynn Stone
Klaus Uhlenhut/Animals Animals
Bob Firth/International Stock

Mammals

MAMMALS EVERYWHERE

Mammals live in a wide variety of habitats. They walk the land, swim the seas, and even take to the air. You are one of them. Like tigers, whales, and bats, people are mammals.

The bat is the only mammal that can fly.

▼ CLOSE TIES
People are part of the mammal group known as primates, which includes apes, monkeys, lemurs, and tarsiers. Primates can walk upright and, with their opposable thumbs, use their hands to pick up things. Some primates have large, complex brains and are very intelligent.

▲ FIRST HERE
Tiny insect-eaters that looked something like today's tree shrew (above) appeared about 195 million years ago in a world that belonged to the dinosaurs. These were the first mammals. Only about 65 million years ago, after most dinosaurs became extinct, did mammals begin to take on a wide variety of shapes and sizes.

TODAY'S COUNT
About 4,000 species of mammals exist today. The squirrel (below) and its rodent relatives make up the largest mammal group—in number of species and number of individual animals.

These apes, known as chimpanzees, are highly intelligent. They've been known to use twigs as tools to dig for termites.

BIG AND SMALL
Mammals come in a wide range of shapes and sizes—from the blue whale (below), more than 100 feet long and weighing 150 tons, to the pygmy shrew, which weighs only 7/100 of an ounce.

▲ **LIVING ALL OVER**

The red fox has the largest range of any carnivore (meat-eater) on Earth. This mammal lives on five continents and hunts in habitats ranging from the edge of the Sahara to the fringe of the northern tundra.

The African elephant is the largest living land mammal, weighing as much as eight tons.

MAMMALS ARE...

All mammals have hair and are warm-blooded, breathe air, and nurse their young.

MILK FOR BABIES ▲
Female mammals, such as this saddleback sow, produce milk in their body to feed their offspring. Young mammals grow quickly on this fat-rich liquid diet.

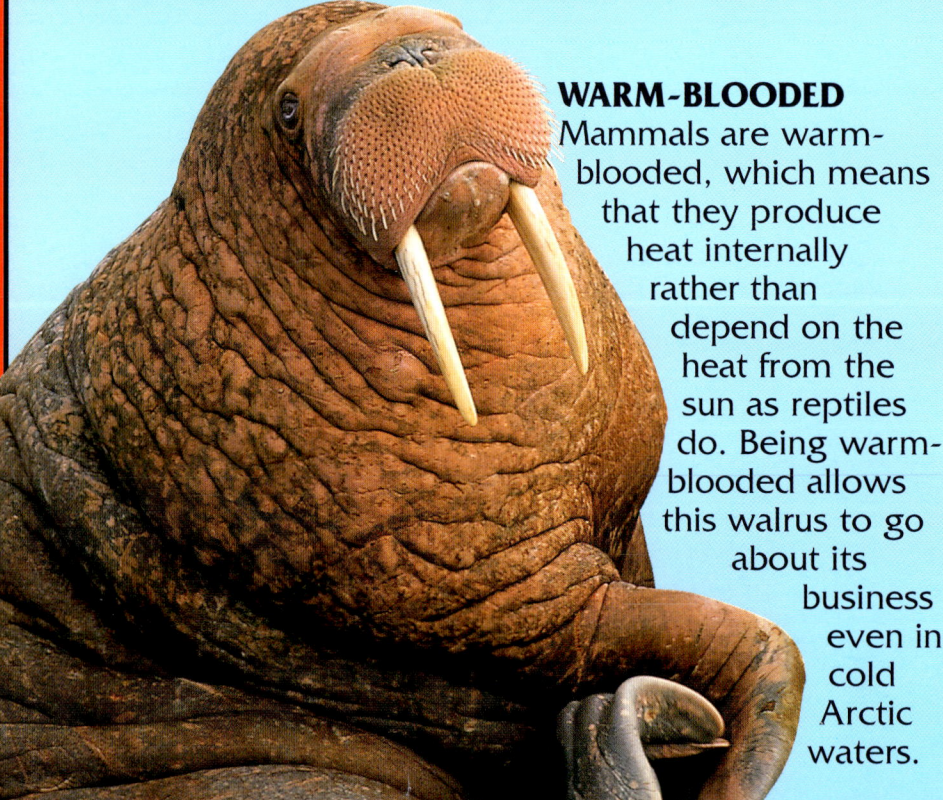

WARM-BLOODED
Mammals are warm-blooded, which means that they produce heat internally rather than depend on the heat from the sun as reptiles do. Being warm-blooded allows this walrus to go about its business even in cold Arctic waters.

HAIR, HAIR
Most mammals have a lot of hair or fur, which helps keep them warm during extremely cold weather. These Japanese macaques, which live in cold, mountain altitudes, enjoy a refreshing dip in a hot spring.

BRAIN POWER ▼
Some mammals are extremely intelligent and good at problem-solving. Dolphins learn easily and can remember complicated series of actions.

▼ BEING BORN
Nearly all mammals give birth to live young. Some mammal babies can get around on their own immediately, but many are helpless and need lots of care. A joey, or baby kangaroo, is hairless and less than one inch long when born. It stays in its mother's pouch, nursing and growing, for six to eight months.

FAMILY TIES
Many mammals have strong family bonds. The relationship between mother and young is often especially close. In a pride of lions, cubs learn how to find food and watch for danger from their mother before going off on their own.

BODIES THAT WORK

Mammals have bodies to suit their lifestyles. Each species has developed specialized body parts for hunting or gathering food, defending itself, and traveling around in its environment.

▼ The long claws of the three-toed sloth are perfect for clamping over tree branches, allowing the sloth to spend most of its life hanging upside down.

TOUGH TEETH ▼

The tiger and other meat-eaters have teeth that are good for holding prey and ripping flesh. Many rodents, such as the coypu (below, right), have large, chisel-like front teeth designed for gnawing.

NIGHT EYES

Nocturnal mammals, such as this galago, have eyes that make the most of even the smallest amounts of light. A reflective layer at the rear of the eye bounces light back to the part of the eye where images are formed.

FINS AND FLIPPERS ▼

If you spend most of your life in the water, as this fur seal does, fins and flippers are more useful than arms and legs. Even on land, a fur seal's flippers work exceptionally well—a large fur seal can gallop faster than a human can run!

HORNS AND ANTLERS

Horns and antlers may be used for defense or in battles between males. Horns, like those of the bighorn sheep, last for the animal's life. They have a core of bone that is covered with keratin—the same material that makes up your fingernails. Antlers are also made of bone, but they do not last the animal's whole life. Each year in the winter, the antlers drop off, and a new set grows in the spring.

▼ A male elk, or moose, which grows as tall as 6 feet at the shoulders and weighs as much as 1,400 pounds, can have antlers that measure up to 5 feet across.

Rocky Mountain bighorn sheep

HANDY TAILS

When you are moving from branch to branch, trying to grab food and hang on at the same time, an extra hand is useful. Some tree-dwelling monkeys, such as this spider monkey, have a strong tail, called a prehensile tail, which bends and can grasp things much the way a hand does.

FROM PLACE TO PLACE

Mammals have adapted to life in all kinds of places—on grassy plains and mountaintops, in desert sands and polar snows.

ON THE PLAINS

Flat, grassy plains are home to grazers, such as zebra (below), wildebeests, and impala. These grass-eaters are fast-moving, hoofed mammals that travel in herds for protection. Because they are prey for lions and other meat-eaters, grazers keep to their herd, especially at a water hole, where they are more likely to be attacked.

UP HIGH

The llama lives on the slopes of South America's Andes Mountains. Its blood has a lot of red blood cells, which are very efficient at collecting oxygen. This enables the llama to cope with the lower oxygen levels found at high altitudes.

UNDER GROUND ▲

The star-nosed mole spends its life underground, where smell may be the most important sense. Each of the 22 tentacles on its snout helps it locate prey in the dark.

▲ TOTALLY TROPICAL
From treetop to jungle floor, 40 square miles of rain forest may hold 125 kinds of mammals, along with many other animals. The jaguar—the largest cat found on the American continents—lives in the tropical forests of South America. It is a good swimmer and has been known to kill crocodiles.

CHILL OUT
The polar bear spends a lot of time traveling over Arctic sea ice on heavily furred, antislip paws. Its thick coat traps air and keeps the bear warm while it searches for food. If the wind is right, the bear can smell a dead seal from 12 miles away.

HOT SPOTS
The camel is built for life in the desert. Its body is very good at conserving water, and its long eyelashes protect its eyes from blowing sand. The pads of a camel's feet spread out to give it traction in the sand.

CITY DWELLERS ▼
Some mammals have adapted quite well to the changes that humans have made in the environment. The house mouse, Norway rat, raccoon, and others make their home in towns and cities.

A deer mouse

THE WET ONES

Even though all mammals need to breathe air, many have evolved to spend life in or near water. Whales and dolphins never leave the sea and can stay underwater for hours at a time. To make breathing easier upon surfacing, they have developed nostrils called blowholes at the top of their head.

◀ **SEA UNICORN**
The 15-foot-long narwhal cruises the cold Arctic waters. In Europe during the Middle Ages, the narwhal's tusk, nearly 10 feet long, was believed to be the horn of the mythical unicorn. In fact, it is just an overgrown front tooth.

COOL TOOL
Webbed feet and a strong tail help the sea otter get around in the ocean. The otter sometimes places a flat rock on its chest and then pounds shellfish on it until the shellfish opens.

THINK PINK ▲
Largest of all river dolphins, the pink river dolphin of South America is about 7 1/2 feet long and weighs up to 280 pounds. Baby river dolphins are dark gray. As they grow older, their skin lightens so that blood vessels beneath the skin can be seen, which gives them a pink coloring.

MERMAID MAMMALS

Sailors' tales of mermaids may have come from glimpses of manatees. These mammals, also called sea cows, live in shallow coastal waters and eat water plants and sea grasses. To deal with this tough food, manatees have intestines more than 145 feet long.

DIP FROM DANGER

The largest living rodent, the capybara, can weigh up to 140 pounds but is a strong swimmer. This resident of South America heads for water at the first sign of danger and can stay under for nearly five minutes to avoid a predator.

MAKE A LAKE

By building dams, the beaver raises the water level around its home, or lodge. This keeps the lodge entrance underwater. The beaver uses the pond that the dam creates to store branches and other food for the winter. The cold water keeps the food from rotting.

RIVER HORSE

Hippopotamus means "horse of the river"—a good name for these large mammals, which leave the water only at night, to eat grass and plants. Spending the day in the water keeps the hippo cool and comfortable.

UNIQUE TREATS

As a group, mammals eat a varied diet, but some individual species have their own ideas about what foods are best.

MMM, ANTS
The anteater, a powerful digger, tunnels into anthills and termite mounds in search of food. It eats insects with the help of its long, sticky tongue, while its tough skin protects it from bug bites.

LEAF EATER ▼
Thanks to its diet, the koala always smells a bit like cough drops. The koala mainly munches the leaves of just five or six kinds of eucalyptus, even though there are about 350 species from which to choose.

◀ FRUIT PLATE
The common palm civet is a catlike mammal that lives in hot, wet areas of Asia. A good climber, it spends much of its time in the trees looking for some of its favorite foods. The civet eats at least 35 kinds of fruit, including some that are poisonous to humans.

IT'S A STRAIN ▼
The humpback whale's favorite food is krill, which is only two to three inches long. The whale strains great mouthfuls of seawater through horny plates, called baleen, that hold back the shrimplike krill for the whale to swallow.

FISHY BEAR
Grizzlies gather along the Pacific Coast when salmon come up the rivers to spawn. They may feast on freshly caught fish or scavenge an easier meal of fish that are already dead.

CLEANING UP
Found throughout much of the Americas, the raccoon is known for ransacking garbage cans and scattering trash in residential communities. It also has a reputation for "washing" its food—exploring the object with its paws—even in the absence of water. The name *raccoon* comes from the Native American word *arakun*, which means "he who scratches with his hands."

ON THE HUNT

Predatory mammals catch their meals in many ways. The cheetah (below), accelerating like a sports car to speeds of up to 70 mph, must catch its prey quickly or give up. It is not built for endurance. Only about half of its chases end with a kill.

▼ TARGET IN SIGHT

Unlike members of the dog family, which rely heavily on their sense of smell to help them find prey, the cougar hunts mainly with its eyes. Once its prey is in sight, the cougar slowly stalks close enough to attack with a few bounding leaps.

PACK ATTACK

Wolves work as a pack to bring down their prey. A wolf pack, which may have 7 to 20 animals, is made up of several pairs of adults and some pups. Hunting as a group allows wolves to catch and kill bigger animals than a single wolf could handle.

WHALE OF A HUNTER

  The orca, also known as the killer whale, is actually the largest of the dolphins. Orcas are fast, intelligent hunters that often work in a group. If they spot seals resting on ice floes, orcas may tip the ice, then catch the seals as they slide off. This orca has thrust itself close to shore to catch its meal.

TUNED IN ▼

Bats use a special kind of sense called *echolocation* to find prey. They send out high-pitched noises, which bounce off objects and return to the bat's ears. This sonar system allows bats to hunt at night for frogs, fish, and insects.

POISONOUS SPIT ▲

  The water shrew swims through streams hunting for small fish, frogs, and crustaceans. When it catches them, a secret weapon helps the little shrew subdue struggling prey: Poisonous saliva flows down grooves in the shrew's teeth and into its prey.

◄ EATING SNAKE

  The mongoose has a reputation for attacking even the largest and most poisonous snakes. Although the mongoose is not immune to a snake's venom, it is very quick and can avoid the lightning-fast strikes of a viper.

ON THE DEFENSE

Mammals use different tactics to avoid being eaten by predators. The snowshoe hare (right) has camouflage that changes with the seasons. In winter, the hare is white to blend in with the snow. In summer, its coat is brown to help it hide in grass and brush.

OUCH!

Porcupines keep their quill-filled rear ends pointed toward a potential attacker. The quills are so loosely attached to the porcupine's skin that even the slightest contact can leave a predator with a painful quill in its face or paw.

TURN AND FIGHT ▼

Weighing up to a ton, an angry Cape buffalo can discourage even the most determined predator. Cape buffalo have been known to charge and chase away attacking lions!

◄ MAKE A STINK

If a striped skunk stamps its front feet and does a handstand, step back and look out! A frightened or angry skunk can spray very smelly fluids, from glands near its tail, up to 10 feet away.

PLAY DEAD ▲
Some predators don't like to eat dead things. The opossum sometimes takes advantage of this by playing dead when a predator comes near. Once the danger has passed, the opossum hurries away.

ON GUARD
Meerkats live in family groups, and sometimes several families live together. Each day as the group forages for food, the meerkats take turn standing guard, watching for possible prey or danger.

RUN FOR IT ▲
On the North American prairie, there are few places to hide. The pronghorn deer relies on its speed to carry it away from danger. It can run at 50 mph for almost a mile, and has been clocked running at 35 mph for more than three miles.

FAMILY CIRCLE
When danger threatens, a herd of musk oxen forms a protective circle, with the calves in the center and the adults facing outward.

23

WEIRD AND WONDERFUL

There are some strange mammals out there. Australia's platypus and echidna are the only two members of a group known as monotremes—egg-laying mammals! Once their babies hatch, they are fed on their mother's milk just like other young mammals.

▲ Echidnas have only one natural enemy—humans!

▲ The platypus is an excellent swimmer. It uses its bill to stir up the river bottom for its meals—worms, shellfish, and insects.

NOT A CARTOON ▼

The real Tasmanian devil is a carnivorous marsupial, or pouched mammal, weighing up to 17 pounds. It lives on Tasmania, an island near Australia. Its strong teeth and jaws are very good for tearing and eating dead animals.

▲ OVERHEAD HOPPERS

The tree kangaroo is good at leaping from one tree to another, but it is rather clumsy on the ground. Compared to its ground-dwelling relatives, it has short back legs, but its long tail helps it stay balanced in the branches.

SCALY

Sometimes described as a "walking pinecone," the giant pangolin of Africa is covered with thick, overlapping scales. The pangolin uses its strong front claws to tear into termite mounds and ant nests. It slurps up the insects with a tongue that may be as long as 28 inches.

LONG NECK

Believe it or not, the giraffe has the same number of bones in its neck as most other mammals. Yet a male giraffe can be up to 18 feet tall, has a 15-inch-long tongue, and can reach high into acacia trees for its leafy meals.

WEAR ARMOR

The 20 species of armadillo carry protection with them. An armadillo's body is covered with hard plates called scutes. When frightened, an armadillo may dig into the ground, crouch, or roll into a ball, leaving only its scutes exposed. That leaves a predator with very little to bite.

THE NOSE KNOWS

The large nose of a male proboscis monkey may be four inches long—long enough to overhang his mouth and get in the way when he eats or drinks. Proboscis females seem to prefer the males with the longest noses.

TROUBLED TIMES

We are in danger of losing some mammals forever, mainly due to overhunting and habitat destruction. Areas where gorillas live in Africa are open to poachers, civil war, and other threats. Some experts estimate that there may be 100,000 gorillas left in Africa. Most are lowland gorillas (below). The mountain gorilla is the most endangered, with perhaps only 600 individuals living in the wild.

FADING BEAUTY
The thick and lovely fur coat of the snow leopard helps it endure the intense cold of Asia's mountains in winter. This mysterious cat is now very rare because it has been hunted—illegally—for its fur.

WHERE ARE THE WHALES?
Humans have hunted whales for meat and oil for a long time. Too much hunting reduced the numbers of some kinds of whales, especially the right whale (above), to dangerously low populations. Pollution also threatens them. Despite this, whaling still continues today.

LOSING LEMURS ▼
Destruction of the forests on the island of Madagascar means that some mammals found nowhere else on earth, such as lemurs, are struggling to survive.

NO MORE RHINOS
A false belief that the horn of the rhinoceros makes a powerful medicine has resulted in these mammals being almost completely wiped out. Conservation officers have removed the horns of some living rhinos, without harming them, in an attempt to keep poachers away.

FERRETS NEED FOOD ▲
The black-footed ferret's homeland is the North American prairie, where it has traditionally preyed upon prairie dogs. But it has become endangered because ranchers have drastically reduced its food supply—prairie dogs. Ranchers believe that the grass-eating prairie dogs are too much competition for their cattle.

◄ GOLDEN MONKEYS
The brilliant coloring of the golden lion tamarin makes it stand out like a beacon in its rain-forest home. But these tamarins are disappearing because of poaching and destruction of the forest. Fewer than 400 of these small monkeys remain in the wild.

Photo Credits: Insects

Bill Beatty: pages 43, 47, 50, 52
Dwight Kuhn: pages 33, 34, 36, 37, 41, 43, 49, 52, 52-53
Tom & Pat Leeson: page 38
Robert & Linda Mitchell: pages 30, 31, 32, 34, 35, 36, 37, 40, 41, 42, 43, 44, 45, 46, 47, 48, 49, 51, 53
A. B. Sheldon: page 51
Lynn M. Stone: page 40
Alabama Bureau of Tourism: page 50
Stanley Breeden/DRK: pages 40-41
Fred Bruemmer/DRK: pages 38-39
D. Cavagnaro/DRK: page 46
Marty Cordano/DRK: page 44
Michael Fogden/DRK: page 39
John Gerlach/DRK: page 52
Stephen J. Krasemann/DRK: pages 33, 40, 45
Sid and Shirley Rucker/DRK: page 39
John Winnie Jr./DRK: page 33
Robert Calentine/Visuals Unlimited: page 48
L. J. Connor/Visuals Unlimited: page 51
John D. Cunningham/Visuals Unlimited: page 30
Carlyn B. Galati/Visuals Unlimited: page 47
Barbara Gerlach/Visuals Unlimited: page 33
Tim Hauf/Visuals Unlimited: page 53
Ken Lucas/Visuals Unlimited: page 32
Steve McCutcheon/Visuals Unlimited: page 48
Kjell B. Sandved/Visuals Unlimited: pages 39, 42
Science VU/Visuals Unlimited: page 44
Leroy Simon/Visuals Unlimited: page 30
Milton H. Tierney Jr./Visuals Unlimited: page 36
Richard Walters/Visuals Unlimited: page 49
William J. Weber/Visuals Unlimited: page 37
Rick & Nora Bowers/Wildlife Collection: page 38
Ken Deitcher/Wildlife Collection: page 41
Charles Melton/Wildlife Collection: page 42

INSECTS

THE WONDER OF INSECTS

We live in a world of insects. Close to one million different species have been identified, making them the most abundant group of creatures on earth. From flies and bees to butterflies, ants, and beetles, insects are found all over the world. One acre of ground may be home to more than a million insects!

ANCIENT INSECTS ▲
Insects have been on Earth for more than 300 million years—since before the days of the dinosaurs! We have found insect fossils (like these termites, trapped in amber) from long ago. Insects were the first creatures to develop wings and fly, which helped them escape from predators and find new places to live.

SHAPES AND SIZES ▲
Some insects are so tiny that you need a magnifying glass or microscope to get a good look at them. Unmagnified, the flea above is just 1/16 of an inch long. Other insects are huge: The African giant swallowtail butterfly is as big as a bird, with a wingspan of six to ten inches.

▼ This insect's name is the banded sphinx moth, or *Eumorpha fasciata*.

TOO MANY TO COUNT
Entomologists (people who study insects) estimate that the one million known insect species are only part of the story. There may be ten times as many that haven't been discovered and named yet!

ALL OVER THE WORLD
Insects live everywhere: at the frozen North and South poles and in blazing-hot deserts; in rivers and lakes; in rain forests and farm fields—even in the biggest cities. Tropical areas are home to many of the largest beetles, butterflies, and ants.

▼ Nobody likes flies, which is probably why we say "Buzz off!" to someone who is *bugging* us!

INSECTS AND PEOPLE
People have been fascinated by insects for a long time. Some we don't like—and some we do! In Japan and China, the symbol for *ant* comes from two other symbols: one that means *insect*, and one that means *unselfishness, justice,* and *courtesy*.

▶ HEY, I'M FLEXIBLE
Insects are experts at finding the right places to live, hide, and eat. Leaf-cutter ants (right) eat fungus that they cultivate on leaves in warm, moist places. They thrive in tropical rain forests. Carpenter ants prefer dry, soft wood, so they are much happier in older, drier forests—or the walls of your house.

▲ AMAZING COLORS
Some of the coolest colors on any living thing belong to beetles. Just look at this rainbow wood-borer! In the Amazon rain forest and elsewhere, people use the colorful outer wing cases of jewel beetles to make necklaces and other jewelry.

31

INSECTS IN THE WEB OF LIFE

Only one percent of all insects are the pesky kind that cause problems. What do all the others do? In nature, all living things are part of the food chain. Insects are a major source of food for millions of different animal species. They do other important work, too.

▲ POLLINATORS

Lots of plants reproduce by making flowers—but the flowers can't make seeds until they get pollinated. Bees, butterflies, moths, and some beetles are pollinators: When they visit a flower to eat, they get covered with pollen, a soft powdery substance. They spread it as they go from flower to flower.

▲ RECYCLERS

Carrion beetles feed on yucky stuff, such as dead animals, fur, and feathers. They help prevent the spread of disease by turning waste materials into fresh new soil that is rich in nutrients. This helps plants grow, making food for other animals.

FISH FOOD
Water bugs, caddis flies, mayflies, and other insects live in or around water. They make great meals for all kinds of fish, as well as for frogs, salamanders, snakes, and other animals that live in or close to streams and lakes.

Giant water bugs carrying their eggs on their backs

32

BIRD FOOD ▶

Insects are food for many of the world's birds. Some swallows and warblers live on nothing but insects. It takes a lot of flies, gnats, and caterpillars to feed a nest of hungry babies, but there are always plenty of insects to go around! One third of all bird species would die off if there were no insects to eat.

▼ BUG EAT BUG

Insects are an important source of food for many animals, including other insects! Ladybugs feed on aphids; hornets and wasps eat caterpillars; ants eat the larvae of beetles and termites; and dragonflies zoom around catching gnats and mosquitoes.

BEAR FOOD

Can you believe that a 500-pound grizzly bear would eat moths? Every summer in some areas of the Rocky Mountains, grizzlies feast on hordes of army cutworm moths, scooping them up in big bunches with their paws. The moths are around for only a few weeks, so the bears gobble up all they can!

▼ YOU AND ONLY YOU

The flower on red clover is so big that most pollinators can't reach its nectar. But a bumblebee has the right stuff. Its massive body lets it burrow all the way in. The bee collects pollen and helps the clover reproduce. This is a special connection in nature between one kind of insect and one kind of plant.

INSECT EQUIPMENT

What makes an insect an insect? How can you distinguish insects from other creepy crawlies? It's not so hard. All of the world's insects have a few things in common.

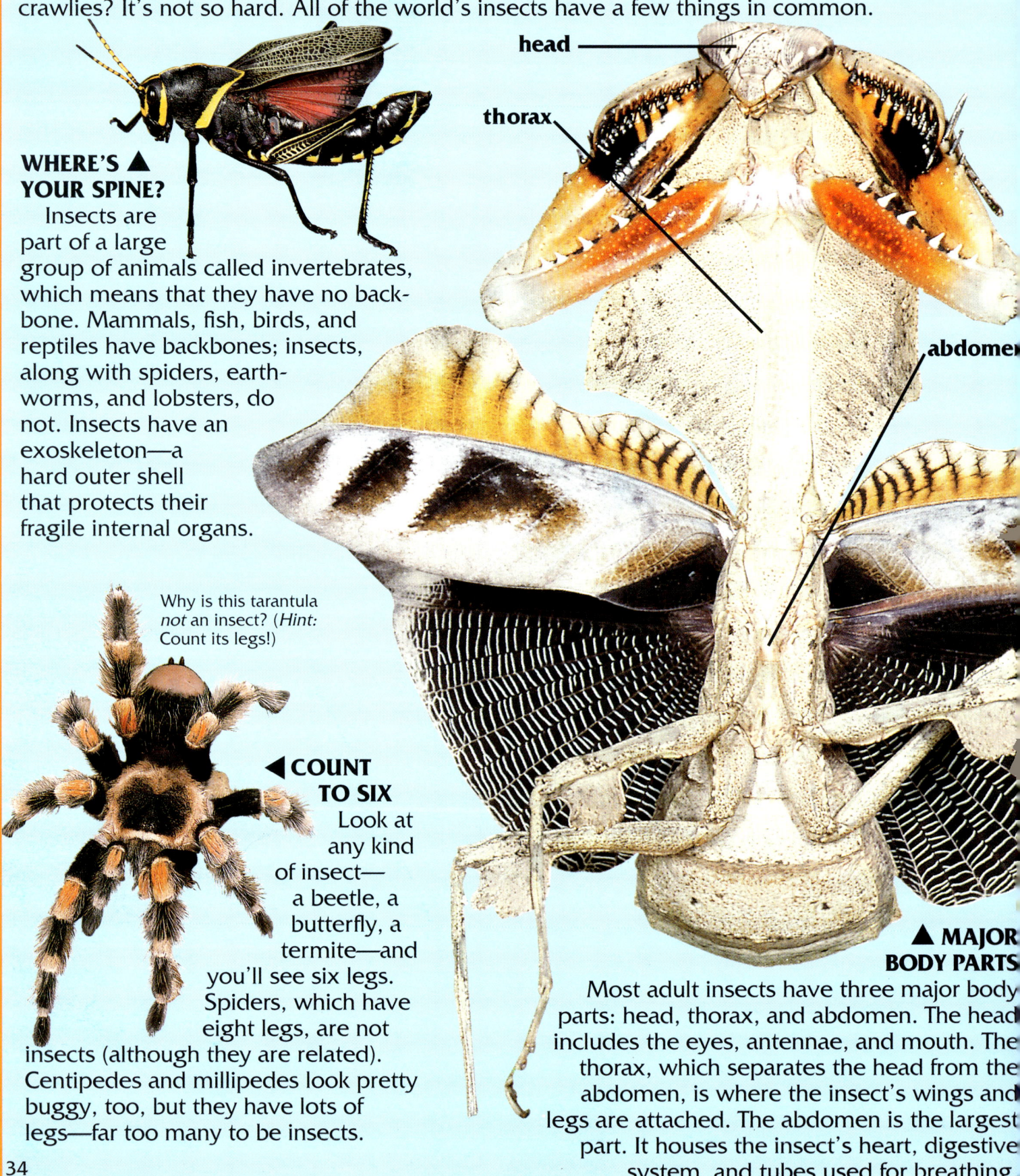

▲ WHERE'S YOUR SPINE?

Insects are part of a large group of animals called invertebrates, which means that they have no backbone. Mammals, fish, birds, and reptiles have backbones; insects, along with spiders, earthworms, and lobsters, do not. Insects have an exoskeleton—a hard outer shell that protects their fragile internal organs.

Why is this tarantula *not* an insect? (*Hint:* Count its legs!)

◀ COUNT TO SIX

Look at any kind of insect— a beetle, a butterfly, a termite—and you'll see six legs. Spiders, which have eight legs, are not insects (although they are related). Centipedes and millipedes look pretty buggy, too, but they have lots of legs—far too many to be insects.

▲ MAJOR BODY PARTS

Most adult insects have three major body parts: head, thorax, and abdomen. The head includes the eyes, antennae, and mouth. The thorax, which separates the head from the abdomen, is where the insect's wings and legs are attached. The abdomen is the largest part. It houses the insect's heart, digestive system, and tubes used for breathing.

◀ EVERY BREATH YOU TAKE

Insects breathe air like other animals, but the way they do it is pretty different. Along the outside of the abdomen are tiny holes called spiracles. They allow air to flow inside the body. Connected to the spiracles are large air sacs and a web of breathing tubes called trachea (TRAY-key-uh).

WINGED WONDERS ▶

Nearly all insects have two pairs of wings. (Flies have only one pair.) Flying allows insects to travel, sometimes for hundreds or thousands of miles. This helps them find new places where food is abundant, find mates for breeding, and escape from predators and harsh weather.

A long-horned beetle about to take flight.

WEIRD BLOOD

Insects have blood (called hemolymph), but it's very different from ours. Usually, it is clear or light green in color. The insect's heart pumps blood, but the blood doesn't flow through arteries or veins, because there aren't any! It just flows freely inside the insect's body.

◀ UP FOR GRABS

The mouth of an insect is adapted to whatever that species eats—whether it chews leaves, sweeps the water for microscopic plants and animals, grabs and cuts into large prey, or bores into the tough wood of trees.

A long-horned wood-borer beetle.

35

A BUG'S LIFE

A baby insect doesn't look much like it will as an adult. It goes through a number of big changes in its lifetime. This process of transformation is called *metamorphosis*, a word that means *a great change in body or appearance.*

COMPLETE METAMORPHOSIS ▶

The most advanced insects—such as butterflies, moths, bees, ants, and flies—undergo *complete metamorphosis*. They start as larvae (hatchlings), then go through a complete change. A caterpillar is a moth or butterfly larva. It turns into a pupa (1). Protected by a tough outer case called a chrysalis (2), the pupa forms legs, wings, and a new body (3). When the change is complete, the insect emerges as an adult—like this monarch butterfly (4)—looking very different from its younger self.

INCOMPLETE ▶ METAMORPHOSIS

Dragonflies, cockroaches, grasshoppers, and stone flies become adults through *incomplete metamorphosis*. The young, called nymphs, molt (shed their skin) many times, growing steadily larger and more like adults. For its final molt, this dragonfly nymph found a rock or branch. Its skin split open, then the adult flew off.

▲ AN EGG START

All insects begin as eggs. Females lay eggs in a sheltered place, such as under the ground, in the bark of a tree or at the bottom of a stream. A wasp laid her eggs inside this caterpillar! When the babies hatched, they fed on the caterpillar, then crawled out to spin cocoons on its back.

1. New pupa
2. Chrysalis (KRIS-uh-lus)
3. Pupa nearing molt
4. Adult emerging

Praying mantis hatchlings

◀ **WHERE ARE MOM AND DAD?**
Most insects grow up without parents around—they hatch and are soon on their way! But termites, ants, some wasps, and honeybees build large nests with special rooms for laying eggs, and spend a lot of time caring for their young. Some beetles also care for their eggs and newly hatched babies.

BUTTERFLIES AND MOTHS

With their awesome colors, shapes and sizes, butterflies and moths are some of the neatest insects around. You know that it's summer when you see them floating over flower gardens, ponds, and fields.

Sheep moth

▲ MOTH OR BUTTERFLY? ▼

How can you tell a moth from a butterfly? Moth antennae are lined with feathery hairs and have no club at the end; butterfly antennae have a small knob at the end. Moths rest with their wings out flat or angled like a tent; when butterflies rest, they fold their wings straight up.

California sisters butterfly

WILD BEAUTIES ▲

There are more than 170,000 kinds of butterflies and moths. They live just about everywhere, from high mountain meadows and cold, windy tundra to tropical rain forests, deserts, and woodlands. These monarch butterflies travel thousands of miles a year: They spend the summer in central and eastern North America, then fly to Mexico for the winter.

DANGEROUS COLORS ▲
Some animals eat butterflies and moths. They have to be careful, though, because some are poisonous. Most poisonous butterflies and moths have bright colors or large eyespots on their wings: warning signs that say *Danger! Stay away!* Some nonpoisonous ones have the same patterns to make other animals think that they, too, are deadly!

▲
WHAT'S IN A WING?
Butterfly and moth wings are made of tiny scales that overlap like shingles on a house. Some scales contain pigments that give moths and butterflies their incredible colors.

SUPER SIPPERS ▶
Adult moths and butterflies don't eat—they drink. They have a flexible, hollow tube, called a proboscis, for a mouth. They extend the proboscis into a flower's blossom, find the nectar, and drink it up, the way you use a straw.

39

HUNTERS AND HUNTED

Every single day, an insect must find enough food while making sure that other animals don't feed on it! But insects have been playing this game for millions of years, and have developed a lot of tricks to help them survive.

▲ SPEED DEMON

The dragonfly is the fastest flier and has the keenest vision of any insect. It can see in almost every direction at once, and keeps its huge eyes clean by using special brushes on its front legs. Zooming after mayflies, mosquitoes, and other small insects, a dragonfly can hit 60 miles per hour! Male dragonflies establish territories and will dive-bomb other males that get too close.

WHO GOES THERE?

Many mild-mannered insects have colors and shapes that make them look dangerous—a trick called mimicry. This deadly-looking "snake" is really a cleverly disguised caterpillar.

▲ ON THE PROWL

The front legs of the praying mantis, or mantid, are serrated for extra gripping power, to hold prey caught in its lightning-fast strike. Its head swivels in every direction, giving it excellent vision. Green or brown mantids blend with their surroundings, but the extra-tricky orchid mantid looks like a flower, drawing other bugs to its clutches.

BARK? TWIG? BUG?

When this northern walkingstick stops moving, it looks like a twig, blending with its surroundings. Moths and butterflies have wing colors that match the leaves or bark of trees—even the shapes of some leaves! When they sit still, birds, rodents, and other predators can't see them!

If a young walkingstick loses a leg, it grows a new one when it molts!

ROW, ROW, ROW

Water striders stay afloat on long legs coated with waxy, waterproof hairs, and use their middle legs like oars to move across water. They live on ponds, rivers, or oceans, eating insects that they find on the water's surface. (They eat each other, too!) They inject their prey with an enzyme that turns its head into mush.

GET OUT OF THE WAY!

When a colony of driver ants swarms through the African forest on a hunting trip, even monkeys and snakes get out of their way! The worker ants kill and devour caterpillars, scorpions, cockroaches, as well as other ants. They are the most ferocious insects in the world, even attacking much larger prey!

This katydid's bigger-than-usual face helps scare away predators.

SEEING, HEARING, SMELLING

Nearly all insects have eyes and ears. Though seeing and hearing are useful, taste and smell are an insect's most important senses. Insects taste and smell the air, ground, and leaves and flowers of plants in order to determine what is and is not safe to eat.

ON YOUR TRAIL ▼

When most ants leave the colony to search for food, they leave a scent trail. The ant touches its abdomen to the ground, releasing a chemical that other ants read with their antennae. Usually, the trail leads to a new source of food—or back home.

▲ A BUG'S-EYE VIEW

Most insects have two large compound eyes, plus three smaller, simple eyes on top of its head. The compound eyes contain hundreds of individual eyes, called facets. Each facet gives the insect a separate picture of the world. You can see the many facets in this fly's eyes (magnified even more in the background photo).

◀ I HEAR YOU CALLING

Hearing is all-important for katydids. There are more than 100 types of katydids in North America and each has its own song, made by rubbing its wings together. Usually, only the males sing. They sing when it's time to mate, to help females find them.

GET THE PICTURE? ▼
The range of colors that many insects see is much different from what humans see. Insects can see ultraviolet, a color that is invisible to us. This may help a bee find the right flowers to feed on, or enable a bluebottle fly to find a mate.

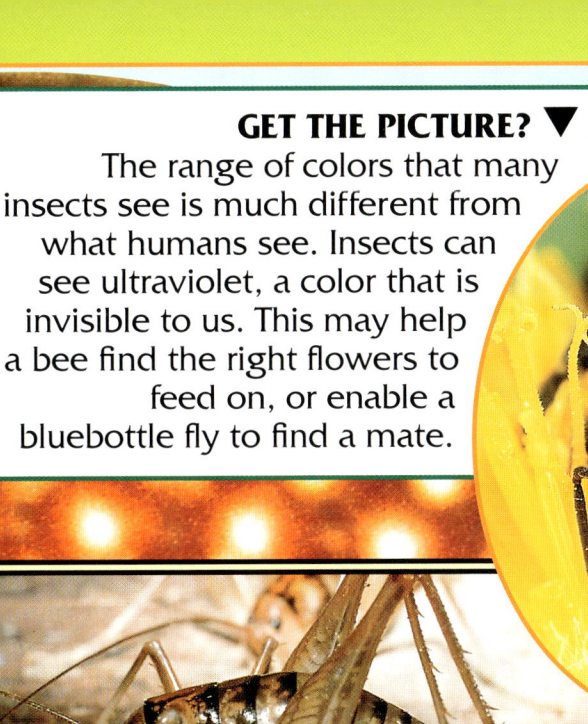

▲ GOOD VIBRATIONS
The cricket has an ear on each front knee! Cricket ears work much like ours: An eardrum picks up vibrations in the air. Other insects have tiny hairs around the eyes and along the body that are sensitive to air movements and other changes in their surroundings.

SHOW ME THE WAY
Fireflies are beetles, not flies. On late summer evenings, firefly males and females put on a show as they locate one another for mating. The male goes first: He sends out a pattern of flashes as he flies, then waits for a female to reply. The light is produced by special cells in the firefly's abdomen.

SNIFFING AROUND
Insects with sharp eyes, such as wasps and dragonflies, have short antennae. Others, such as some beetles and moths (like this luna moth), have long antennae covered with tiny hairs. The antennae pick up smells in the air—from as far as 10 or 12 miles away! That makes smelling as good as seeing: They can find food, safety, and mates by smelling them!

MEET THE BEETLES

With about 300,000 different species known today, beetles make up one fourth of all the world's animal life! Beetles have super-tough exoskeletons; they can fly and dig burrows; some can swim. Their colors, sizes, and mouths are adapted to where they live.

▲ **CLEAN-UP CREW**
The world would be a lot smellier without dung beetles! They consume huge amounts of dung—droppings from cows, buffalo, elephants, and other animals. Some females roll it into a tightly packed ball, then lay their eggs in it.

▲ **FOLD-UP WINGS**
Most insects have four wings, but beetle wings are different. Instead of being light and flexible, a beetle's front wings are hard, almost like a shell. At rest, the hard wings—called elytra (ELL-uh-truh)—fold tightly over the other set of wings like a cover. When the beetle gets ready to fly, the elytra open so the flying wings can unfold and swing out.

HORNS AND JAWS
Some male beetles have enormous jaws and horns. When it's time to defend their territory or battle for a mate, these fellows get mean, pushing and jousting. The fight usually ends when one beetle gets knocked to the ground from a tree limb or log.

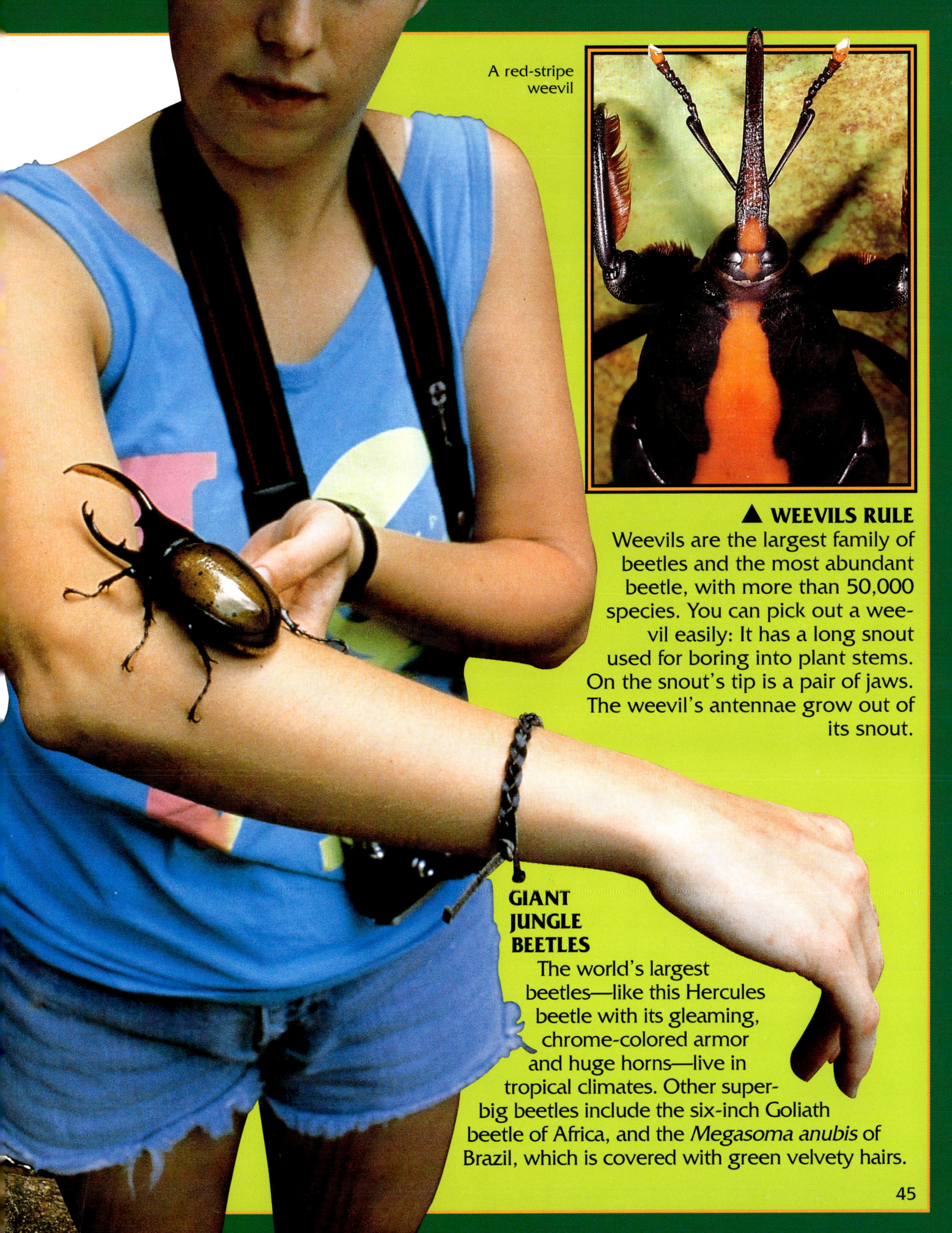

A red-stripe weevil

▲ **WEEVILS RULE**
Weevils are the largest family of beetles and the most abundant beetle, with more than 50,000 species. You can pick out a weevil easily: It has a long snout used for boring into plant stems. On the snout's tip is a pair of jaws. The weevil's antennae grow out of its snout.

GIANT JUNGLE BEETLES
The world's largest beetles—like this Hercules beetle with its gleaming, chrome-colored armor and huge horns—live in tropical climates. Other super-big beetles include the six-inch Goliath beetle of Africa, and the *Megasoma anubis* of Brazil, which is covered with green velvety hairs.

SOCIAL INSECTS

Most insects live on their own, coming together only when it's time to mate. But ants, honeybees, some wasps and hornets, and termites are social insects. They build large colonies, and each member has a job to do.

PAPIER-MÂCHÉ
A single paper-wasp queen starts a new colony each year. She chews up softened wood to make a soft, papier-mâché-like material for the nest. She lays eggs and raises the first worker wasps on her own. Then the workers, all females, take over. On hot days, they cool the nest by fanning their wings, or collecting water to spread over eggs and larvae.

SHAKE IT! ▶
Social insects need to know many things, such as where food is and whether danger is near. Honeybees perform a "dance" to let other worker bees know where nectar is. The dance provides important information—such as the direction, distance, and quantity of the nectar source.

DEFENDING THE COLONY ▶

For insects, protecting eggs and larvae from danger is job #1. If a predator threatens, worker ants scoop up their offspring and race off while soldier ants attack with biting jaws. Some soldier termites squirt a sticky goo at their enemies. Wasps and hornets swarm and sting when they smell an attack hormone released by other workers. *Yeeoww!*

▲ ALL HAIL THE QUEEN

All social insect colonies have a queen. Usually, she is larger than other members of the colony, and the only one able to lay eggs. The termite queen's abdomen becomes so swollen with eggs that she can hardly move!

HIGH-RISE HOMES

Compass termites live in Australia. They build huge, wedge-shaped mounds using soil and their own sticky secretions. Some of these towers stand 15 feet or higher and are just about waterproof. The narrow ends at the top of each mound always face north and south. If you're lost in the Australian outback, find one of these mounds and use it like a compass!

GOOD AND BAD INSECTS

There are many kinds of helpful insects. Bees produce honey and wax, silkmoth caterpillars make silk for clothing, and—for some people—insects make a nutritious, good-tasting meal! There are bad-guy bugs, too: a few kinds that make plenty of trouble for humans. It's never easy to stop them, but we keep trying!

TIMBER!

Many kinds of insects—including grasshoppers (pictured), beetles, and moths—eat the bark, leaves, and wood of trees. The larvae of spruce and pine beetles (called grubs) bore into the trunk of a living tree, weakening or killing it. Grasshoppers are defoliators, which means that they eat a tree's leaves, not the bark or wood.

STRANGE FRUIT ▲

The tiny fruit fly is one of the biggest pests in the world. Females lay eggs beneath the skin of fruits and vegetables. The larvae, called maggots, hatch soon after. The Mexican fruit fly attacks 50 different kinds of fruits and vegetables; the Mediterranean fruit fly attacks more than 250!

GOT SILK? ▶

Ever wonder why silk costs so much? It comes from specially bred and fed silkworms. Each silkworm cocoon is made of a single thread about 1,000 yards long. That thread must be carefully unwound and processed.

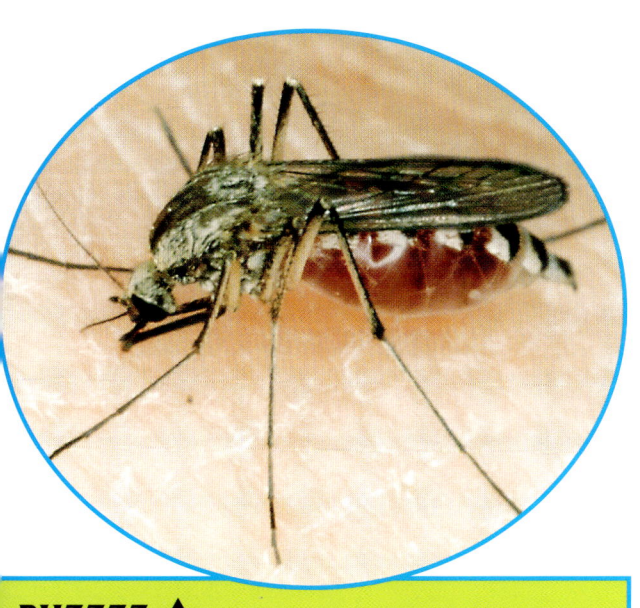

AS BUSY AS CAN BEE
From morning until dusk in summer, honeybees visit flowers. A single bee makes as many as 24 trips a day, and must stop at 100 to 1,500 flowers to fill itself with nectar. A fully loaded bee carries enough nectar to make one drop from an eyedropper. With enough bees, it all adds up: Two hives can make 150 pounds of honey in a year.

BUZZZZ ▲
There are more than 2,500 kinds of mosquitoes. Male mosquitoes eat nectar; only females drink blood. Besides spoiling outdoor fun, their bite can spread such fatal diseases as malaria and yellow fever to humans.

MAY I HELP YOU? ▶
Praying mantises help us out by doing what comes naturally—eating other bugs. The ones they like to eat are usually the same kinds that wreck crops and gardens. (They also enjoy a tasty lizard or frog now and then!)

INSECTS GET AROUND!

Insects are always looking for new places to live. They get into clothes and food shipments, airplanes and boats, luggage and boxes. Wherever people go, insects go, too. There is no way to stop them.

◀ PEST FROM OUT WEST

Long ago, the Colorado potato beetle ate only wild plants. But when American settlers moved west and began farming, it switched to the leaves of potato and tomato crops. No bug-killing chemical has stopped it yet. The beetle has taken hold across Europe and Asia, and recently showed up in China and Iran.

COTTON MENACE ▼

The boll weevil entered Texas (from Mexico) in 1892 and expanded its range by 60 miles each year. By 1922, it was destroying cotton fields throughout Alabama, Georgia, and other southeastern states. But it's a hero in Enterprise, Alabama: A statue honors it for forcing farmers there to switch to crops that turned out to be more profitable.

▲ FROM CANADA

European skipper butterflies came to the U.S. from Canada about 80 years ago. You can now find their plump, furry bodies and brown-orange wings throughout New England. Another new population is growing out west in Colorado and British Columbia. Butterfly experts believe that they may have hitched a ride on a shipment of hay.

NO KILLERS ▼
"Killer bees" are really African honeybees. Beekeepers took them to Brazil—then they escaped, breeding with other bees as they moved north. African bees are quick to defend their hives, but rarely attack people. Africanized bees make great honey. If you have a jar of honey at home, there's a good chance it was made by them.

THE CITY PEST ▼
Cockroaches, also called palmetto bugs, have been around for 280 million years. They are so tough that one can live for nearly three days *without its head*! Cockroaches live by the millions in urban areas, feeding on food scraps and other debris. They are *very* fast and can squeeze into the smallest spaces.

THEY'RE EVERYWHERE
The cabbage butterfly is now so plentiful in the U.S. that it's hard to believe it's a relative newcomer. A native of England, it somehow got to Canada, where it took wing and spread throughout North America. The caterpillars feed on sour-tasting stuff—cabbage, peppergrass, and wild mustard—so it's no wonder birds don't like to eat them!

A BALANCING ACT

The natural world is one big balancing act—and insects are a vital part of it. Studying insects is a great way to learn about nature, because insects are easy to find. Be a bug detective: All you need is a jar with a lid, a magnifying glass, and a pair of tweezers for holding insects you want to study.

An earwig.

A BUG EXPERIMENT

Want to find out how quickly insects adapt to change? Set a large flat rock, log, or piece of wood somewhere in your yard. Every day, go lift it up. What insects are under there? Where did they come from? How did they find out about that place? Why do they like living there?

COME AND GET IT! ▼

If you really like butterflies and want to watch them, ask your parents about planting a butterfly garden. There are certain types of flowers that butterflies can't resist—ask at a garden store. Plant a few of them, then see how many kinds of butterflies visit.

OUR CHANGING WORLD ▲
Many insects have adapted to one kind of *habitat* (natural home). People need homes, too, so every year a little more of the world's rain forests are cleared away. Birds, insects, and other rain-forest animals become extinct—and we lose some of what helps to preserve a delicate balance.

LEARNING MORE ▲
Almost everyone knows what a cockroach looks like, but what about a tiger beetle (above) or a camel cricket? If you want to learn more about insects, buy a field identification guide. You'll see pictures of insects that live in your area, along with notes on where they live and what they eat.

OUT OF BALANCE
Why is it so hard to keep insects from damaging crops? Because a field of crops isn't like a forest or meadow, where many different plants and animals live. A crop field has just one kind of plant and few animals. If a bad bug moves in, there are often no predators to eat it—and no other kinds of plants for that bug to eat. Crop fields don't have balance.

KEEPING THE BALANCE
Why care about insects—yellow jackets like these, for instance? Without these wasps to eat caterpillars, we might not have some of our favorite flowers, because the caterpillars would destroy them. We need many different kinds of plants and animals to keep nature in balance.

Photo Credits: Reptiles & Amphibians

Thomas C. Boyden: pages 60, 72
Kit Kittle: pages 57, 68, 69, 76
Lynn Rogers: pages 62, 63, 74, 75, 76, 77
Anita Baskin-Salzberg: pages 74, 77
Allen Salzberg: pages 74, 77
Michael Fogden/DRK: page 79
William Leonard/DRK: pages 78, 79
Gail Shumway/FPG: page 78
Paul E. Clark/NE Stock Photo: page 58
Art Phaeuf/NE Stock Photo: page 68
Mark Picard/NE Stock Photo: page 66
Photo Researchers: page 62
R. W. Brooks/Photo Researchers: page 71
Miguel Castro/Photo Researchers: page 71
Stephen Dalton/Photo Researchers: page 72
Gregory Dimijian/Photo Researchers: page 63
Brian Enting/Photo Researchers: page 73
Joyce Photographics/Photo Researchers: page 57
Jeffrey W. Lang/Photo Researchers: page 61
Michael McCoy/Photo Researchers: page 64
Tom McHugh/Photo Researchers: pages 59, 63, 65, 68, 72, 73, 74, 75
Lawrence E. Naylor/Photo Researchers: page 65
J. H. Robinson/Photo Researchers: page 67
K. H. Switik/Photo Researchers: pages 57, 70
H. A. Thornhill/Photo Researchers: page 62
Walt Anderson/Visuals Unlimited: page 58
W. A. Banaszewski/Visuals Unlimited: page 60
R. Calentine/Visuals Unlimited: page 65
Nathan W. Cohen/Visuals Unlimited: pages 56, 64, 65
John Cunningham/Visuals Unlimited: pages 63, 70
Don W. Fawcett/Visuals Unlimited: page 57
William Grenfell/Visuals Unlimited: page 70
A. Kerstitch/Visuals Unlimited: page 66
David Matherly/Visuals Unlimited: page 70
Joe McDonald/Visuals Unlimited: pages 66, 69
Jim Merli/Visuals Unlimited: pages 56, 63, 64, 70
Gary Meszaros/Visuals Unlimited: page 78
Tom J. Ulrich/Visuals Unlimited: pages 61, 72
Rod Canham/WaterHouse: page 57

Illustrations:
Crystal Palette: pages 67, 68, 75, 76, 77

Reptiles and Amphibians

REMARKABLE REPTILES

Millions of years ago reptiles dominated the land, sea, and sky. Most of these ancient reptiles—including the dinosaurs—suddenly died out about 65 million years ago. No one knows exactly why. However, five different groups of their ancestors—snakes, crocodilians, lizards, turtles and tortoises, and the tuatara—about 6,500 different species in all, adapted to the changing world and survive today on every continent except Antarctica.

Sun Seekers

Reptiles have thick, scaly skin which prevents their bodies from drying out. The scales are made from keratin, the same material found in your fingernails and hair. The body temperature of these cold-blooded creatures depends on their surroundings. It goes up in warm weather and down in cold weather.

The heat from the sun warms the blood of this basking crocodile.

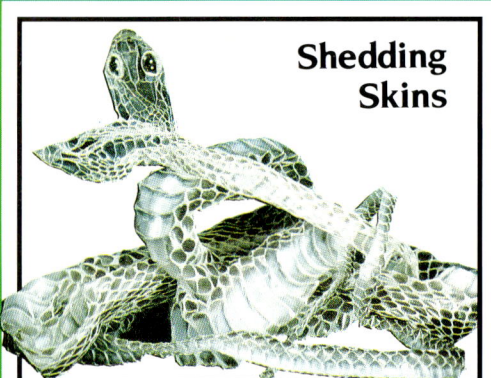

Shedding Skins

Most reptiles keep growing throughout their lives. Snakes and some lizards are able to shed their scaly outer layer of skin as they outgrow it. Lizard skin falls off in flakes but snakes shed their entire skin—sometimes unbroken—at one time.

Lots of Lizards

Lizards come in many sizes and colors, and some, like Jackson's chameleon, even have horns! A chameleon's eyes move independently of each other and in any direction. This allows it to search for food and avoid being eaten at the same time.

Turtles, crocodilians, and most snakes and lizards are hatched from eggs. Reptiles build nests of rotting plant material or dig holes in the warm sand or soil where they deposit their eggs. Some snakes and lizards are born live from eggs that hatch in their mother's body.

When they are ready to hatch, baby reptiles use a special pointed egg tooth or spike located on their snouts to chisel through the shell. Soon after, the egg tooth falls off. The hatchlings are identical to their parents—only smaller.

The Ancient One ▼
Lizard-like in appearance, the tuatara can trace its ancestors back to the time before dinosaurs roamed the Earth. The only survivors of this ancient group of reptiles live on a few islands near New Zealand.

Life In A Shell
The turtle's hard protective shell has enabled it to survive on Earth for over 250 million years. However, some sea turtles have developed a smoother, lighter, more streamlined shell, helping them to better adapt to life in the ocean.

CROCODILIANS

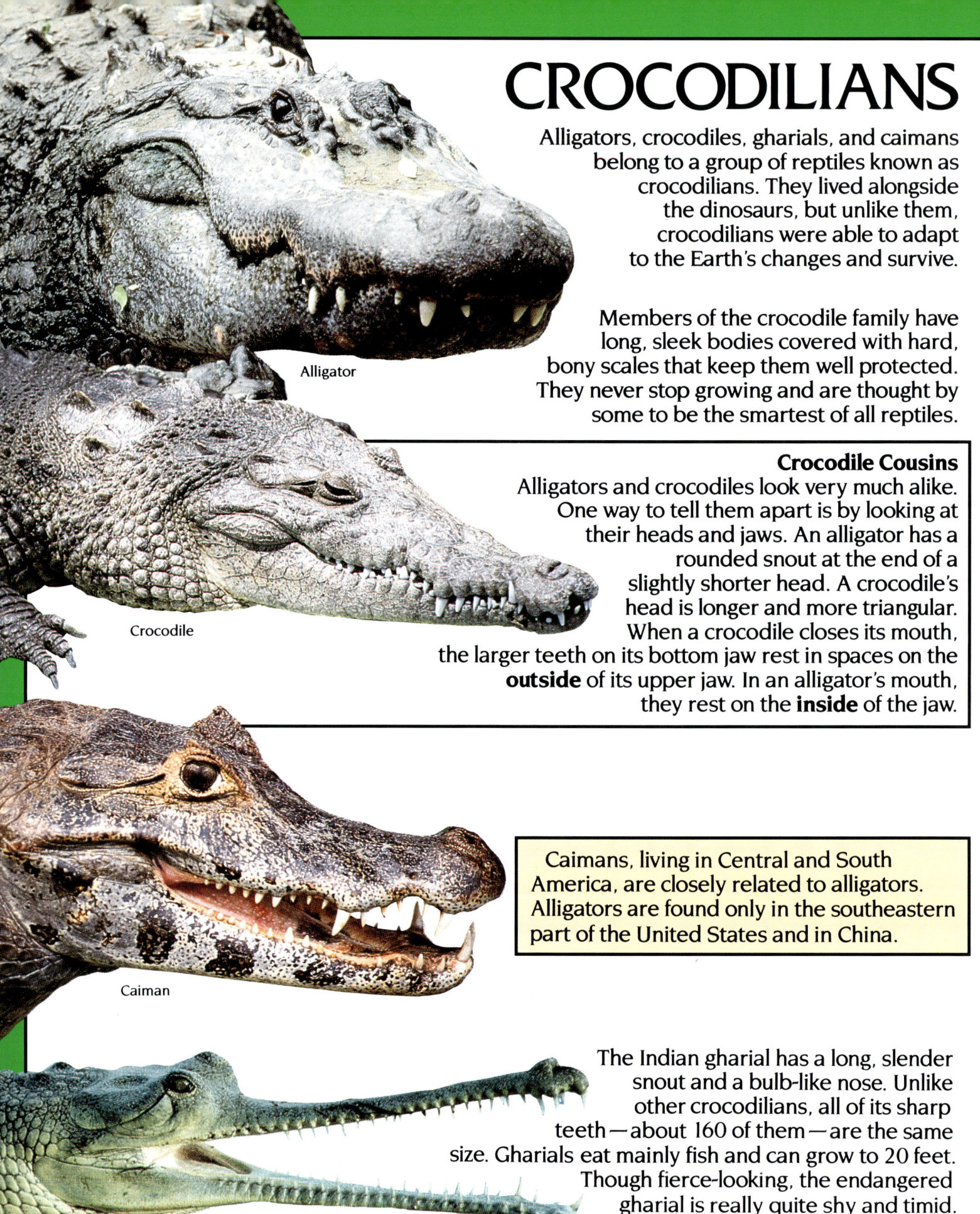

Alligators, crocodiles, gharials, and caimans belong to a group of reptiles known as crocodilians. They lived alongside the dinosaurs, but unlike them, crocodilians were able to adapt to the Earth's changes and survive.

Members of the crocodile family have long, sleek bodies covered with hard, bony scales that keep them well protected. They never stop growing and are thought by some to be the smartest of all reptiles.

Crocodile Cousins
Alligators and crocodiles look very much alike. One way to tell them apart is by looking at their heads and jaws. An alligator has a rounded snout at the end of a slightly shorter head. A crocodile's head is longer and more triangular. When a crocodile closes its mouth, the larger teeth on its bottom jaw rest in spaces on the **outside** of its upper jaw. In an alligator's mouth, they rest on the **inside** of the jaw.

Caimans, living in Central and South America, are closely related to alligators. Alligators are found only in the southeastern part of the United States and in China.

The Indian gharial has a long, slender snout and a bulb-like nose. Unlike other crocodilians, all of its sharp teeth—about 160 of them—are the same size. Gharials eat mainly fish and can grow to 20 feet. Though fierce-looking, the endangered gharial is really quite shy and timid.

A Watery Life

Crocodilians are built for a life in and around water. They are strong swimmers — wiggling through the water with their powerful tails propelling them forward. When floating, the eyes, ears, and nostrils, positioned higher than the rest of the head, are exposed above the water. But when underwater, where they can remain for over an hour, transparent shields slide across their eyes to protect them.

Saltwater Crocodile

Beware That Smile

Silently gliding forward, eyes steady and riveted, the crocodile is a fearsome and aggressive hunter. It will attack large animals and is very dangerous to humans. Alligators, on the other hand, are shy. They will bite if disturbed but most likely will swim or run away when approached.

Record Breakers

Adult male crocodiles measuring over 14 feet are not uncommon, but the all-time champions of size are the saltwater crocodiles of southeast Asia which sometimes stretch out to more than 20 feet.

▶ This crocodile enjoys a peaceful float, but don't be fooled… he's got an eye out for any intruders.

Underwater Dining

Crocodilians cannot chew their food—they swallow it whole. If their prey is too large, they grab it with their sharp teeth, drag it underwater until it drowns, then rip it into chunks with powerful twists of their bodies. A throat flap keeps the water out of their lungs when diving, so they can swallow their food underwater.

A crocodile continually grows new sets of teeth to replace the ones lost while hunting. It can go through about fifty sets in a lifetime!

Powerful Jaws

With one snap an alligator's jaws are powerful enough to cut a large animal in two. However, the muscles which open its mouth are so weak that once shut the alligator's mouth can easily be held together.

All crocodilians are flesh eaters and feed on any animals they can catch — from birds and fish to zebras or antelope. Gharials eat mainly fish. Some crocodilians swallow small stones which help to grind their food and also enable them to float low in the water.

Lazy Day ▶

Much of this crocodile's day is spent basking in the warm sun. At dusk it will perk up and begin hunting for its dinner.

Alligator Nest

Nests and Babies

Female crocodiles dig a hole into which they deposit their eggs in two or three layers before covering them with sand. Alligators prepare rounded nests of mud and decaying vegetation above the ground. Both nests protect the eggs as the sun's warmth incubates them. Unlike most other reptiles, crocodilian mothers guard their nests and stay close to their babies after they are born.

This crocodile is not eating her eggs. Her babies are ready to be born and she's gently rubbing the shells so that they may be released.

Squeak! A saltwater crocodile, 12 inches long and weighing five ounces, emerges from its shell. As an adult it can measure 20 feet and weigh as much as 2,000 pounds.

◀ A mother alligator carries her babies to the water on her back—sometimes in her mouth—as carefully as a mother dog carries her puppies. The hatchlings are miniature versions of their parents.

SNAKES...

Although lacking legs, eyelids, and outer ears, snakes have managed to survive and prosper for more than 135 million years. About 2,800 species of snakes are alive today. Multi-patterned and colored, snakes make their homes on land, in water, underground, and in trees.

New Skin

A snake is not slimy—its scaly skin is dry and smooth. The outer layer of a snake's skin cannot stretch, so when a snake grows too big for its skin it simply develops a new one. This blue racer has broken through its old skin and will soon crawl out with shiny new scales.

Snakes are not vegetarians. They prefer to dine on birds, lizards, mammals, other snakes, frogs, eggs, earthworms, and insects. By unhinging its jaws, a snake is able to swallow large prey—larger than the size of its mouth. ◄This slender garter snake has hunted down a toad, which has puffed itself up to try to prevent from being swallowed.

◀ Sensitive Tongues
A snake flicks out its long, forked tongue to touch and smell. This viper uses its sensitive tongue to scan the area for prey. A snake can follow a scent very well — smelling with its tongue.

Unusual Mother ▼
A python lays between 15 and 100 eggs and is the only snake that helps them hatch. By coiling around her eggs and vibrating her body, this Indian python not only protects them, but keeps the eggs warm and speeds up the hatching.

▲ The common garter snake is found throughout the United States. Unlike most snakes, garter babies are born live, usually in litters of 50 to 60.

◀ Camouflage
A snake's color and scale pattern helps it to blend in with its surroundings. The beautiful coloring of this emerald tree boa helps camouflage it from both predator and prey amongst the leafy canopy of the South American rain forest.

▶ These eastern hognosed snakes have chiseled through their leathery shells with their egg teeth. However, in no hurry to enter the world, they will stay inside the safety of their shells for a day or two before crawling out.

Born to Swim
All snakes can swim and some have chosen to live at sea rather than on land. Sea snakes thrive in the warm waters of the Indian and Pacific Oceans and are extremely poisonous. These swift swimmers can stay underwater for several hours before coming up for air. Sea snake babies are born live at sea.

...AND MORE SNAKES

Most snakes are non-poisonous. They capture their meals by suffocating their prey or by simply biting and gripping them with their sharp teeth. Then, snakes use their large, extended mouths and flexible bodies to swallow their victims. Snakes do not chew — they swallow their food whole and slowly digest it. After a large meal, a snake can go for many months without eating again.

These tree boas aren't having a conversation. They're just hanging out on their favorite branches. Heat sensors along their lips help them detect the tree-dwelling prey on which they feed.

Giant Snake ▼

Constrictors are thick, long, and heavy. South American anacondas easily grow longer than 20 feet and weigh over 500 pounds. One huge anaconda measured 28 feet and weighed in at an incredible 1,100 pounds. This constrictor could swallow a jaguar — whole!

Deadly Embrace

Boas, pythons, and anacondas are constrictors — snakes that suffocate their prey. After seizing a bird in its jaws, this diamond python wraps its body around it and slowly tightens the coils each time the bird exhales. Soon the bird can no longer breathe and finally dies. The constrictor then swallows it whole, digesting everything except the feathers.

▲ Patience
On a branch high above the ground, this slender Central American vine snake tries to imitate a tree limb. A vine snake can stay perfectly still for hours, hoping to fool a bird or lizard into thinking it's just another vine…until, gulp! it's too late to get away.

Look Alikes ▶
The harmless scarlet king snake's unusual coloring makes it look like the deadly coral snake. But remember: "Red touches black, venom lack. Red touches yellow, kills a fellow."

Coral Snake   King Snake

◀ Egg Snatcher
An egg-eating snake can stretch its mouth very wide and slowly move its jaws over an egg. It can swallow eggs twice as wide as its body! Sharp bones in the snake's throat crack and crush the egg, allowing it to swallow the liquid part and spit out the shell.

▲ The Great Pretender
Upon encountering an enemy, the harmless hognosed snake puffs out its neck, hisses, and pretends to strike. If this act fails, it turns over onto its back and plays dead.

Big Ball ▼
When threatened, the African ball python tucks in its head and coils itself into a tight, round ball, which incredibly, can be rolled… but not bounced!

DEADLY FANGS

Of the approximately 650 poisonous snakes, about 250 are dangerous to humans. When a poisonous snake bites, special glands pump venom through its hollow fangs and inject the poison into its victim.

PIT VIPER CLOSE-UP

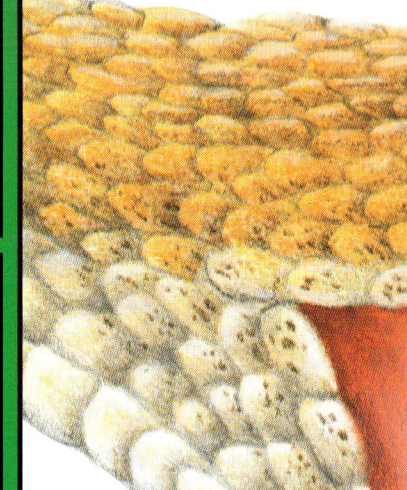

◀ The muscular body of the rare, yellow eyelash viper helps it move easily through the dense tropical forest. Tree-dwelling snakes drink the moisture that collects on leaves.

Venomous Vipers

A viper keeps its extra-long fangs folded back against the roof of its mouth—until it's ready to strike. Vipers have wide heads in which they store their large venom glands. Gaboon vipers, found in tropical African forests, have the longest fangs—up to two inches—of any snake.

Gaboon Viper

Pit Vipers

Some vipers have pits — small holes—one on either side of their faces. These heat-sensing organs help the viper locate prey, especially at night.

▼ The best known pit viper is the rattlesnake. The rattle on the end of its tail is made up of dry, hard pieces of unshed skin. When shaken, the rattle makes a whirring, buzzing sound, warning strangers to stay away.

Copperhead ▲
The copperhead's markings allow it to blend in with the dead leaves on the forest floor. Although painful, this pit viper's bite is rarely fatal to humans.

Can you guess why I'm called a rhinoceros viper?

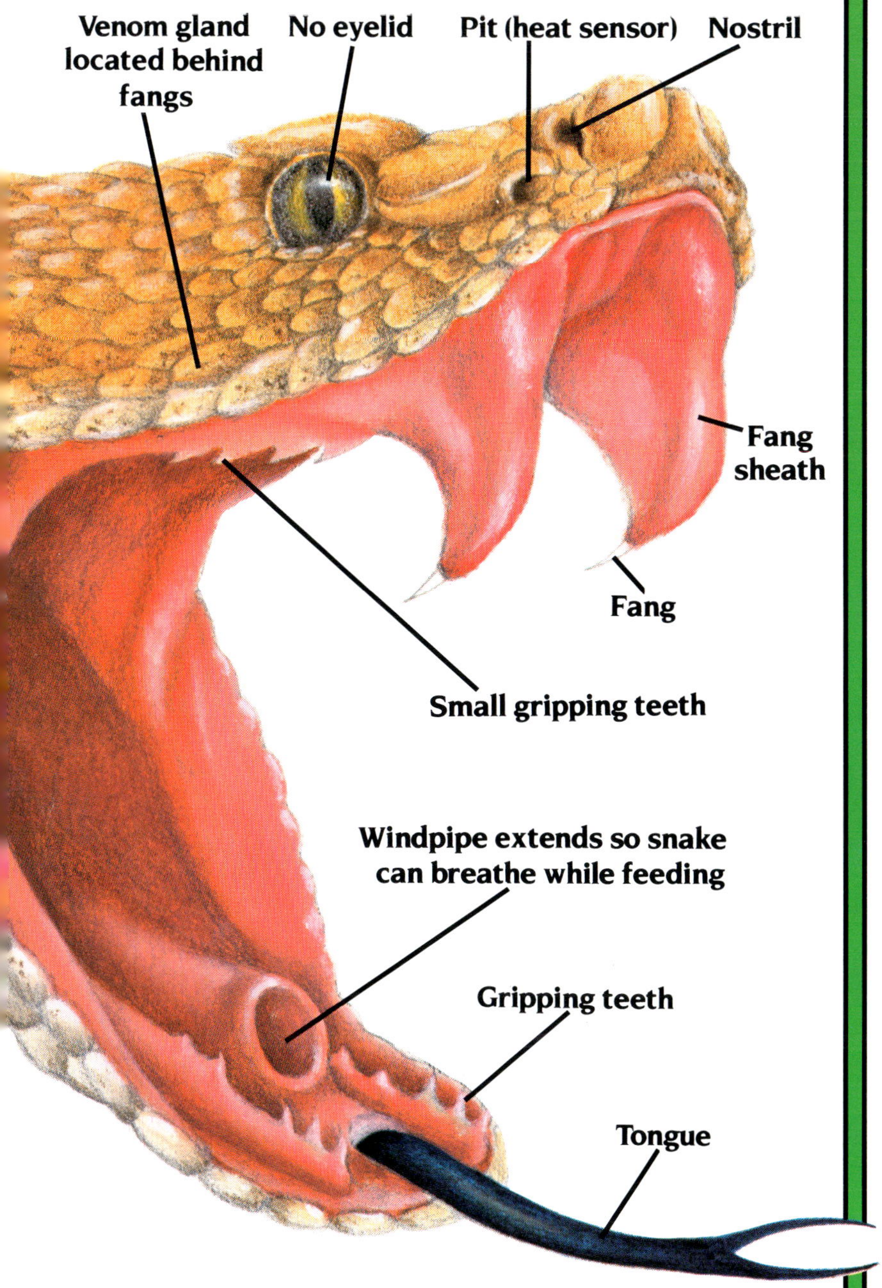

Venom gland located behind fangs
No eyelid
Pit (heat sensor)
Nostril
Fang sheath
Fang
Small gripping teeth
Windpipe extends so snake can breathe while feeding
Gripping teeth
Tongue

Coral Snake

Fixed Fangs
Unlike vipers, the colorful coral snake, along with its cobra, mamba, and sea snake relatives, has two short, sharp fangs fixed at the front end of its upper jaw.

Baby Cobras

Hooded Terror ▲
The 18-foot king cobra is the longest poisonous snake in the world, with venom powerful enough to kill an elephant. When threatened, it spreads the loose skin on its neck into a "hood" several times wider than its body. Moving with its upper body raised off the ground, a hooded cobra is indeed a fearsome sight!

Aggressive baby cobras, armed with fangs and venom, will strike while still emerging from their shells.

Speed Demon ▶
The fast and deadly black mamba can move at a speed of seven miles per hour. It travels with one third of its 10 to 14 foot-long body lifted off the ground and can strike at the level of a person's head. Just two drops of venom from this African snake can kill a human in ten minutes!

LIZARDS

With over 3,500 different species, lizards are by far the largest group of reptiles. They range in size from an inch-long gecko to the 10 foot-long Komodo dragon, and come in many shapes and colors.

Australian Blue-Tongued Skink

Tree-dwelling Chameleon

Sensitive Tongues

Lizards extend or flick their tongues to help them "sense" their environment. The information gathered tells them the whereabouts of food and mates, and warns them of the presence of enemies. But their tongues have other uses, too.

A tree-dwelling chameleon is the "marksman" of the reptile world. Its tongue, kept rolled up in its mouth, is as long or longer than its body. When the chameleon spots an insect, it shoots its sticky tongue out, and zap! — instant lunch.

The Australian blue-tongued skink sticks out and waves its fat blue tongue to frighten away its enemies.

◀ Geckos use their long tongues to clean their faces — including their eyes.

Masters of Disguise

Many lizards have a well known ability to change color. They can match their surroundings to hide from both prey and predator. But first prize for color change goes to the chameleon, who can even change its color to suit its mood.

This chameleon has no trouble blending in with the sunlit foliage of its east African home.

Natural Camouflage

Touch this branch and you've moved an almost-impossible-to-detect giant gecko.

A Tale Of Tails

Many lizards possess the amazing ability to shed their tails when attacked. Incredibly, the dropped tail keeps wriggling, distracting the enemy and giving the lizard a chance to escape. But the lost tail is not missed for long because a lizard can grow another one! Sometimes, if only part of the tail has come off, a lizard, like this skink above, will wind up with two tails.

The bright blue tail of a young skink below draws an enemy's attention away from its body. Better to lose your tail than your life!

Worm? Or Lizard?

Lizards without legs look a lot like small snakes — or huge worms. The worm lizard spends most of its time underground where legs aren't necessary. Moving forward or backward, it hunts for insects and, you guessed it, worms.

◀ Heads Or Tails?

The shingleback or double-headed lizard of Australia really has only one head. But its fat, head-shaped tail makes it look like it has two. This confuses its enemies and, hopefully, causes them to attack the wrong end.

Leopard Gecko

Eggs and Babies

Like their snake cousins, some lizards are born live, but most mothers simply lay their eggs and walk away.

This female leopard gecko had just laid her eggs in a shallow nest. The eggs, soft and sticky, will harden during the months they take to hatch.

Its mother long gone, this green iguana emerges from its leathery shell, ready to fend for itself.

▼ The female North American five-lined skink is one of the few lizards that guards its eggs and cares for its young until they can survive on their own.

Iguana Iguana

Iguanas, the most common lizards living in Central and South America, come in many shapes, sizes, and colors. They live in forests and deserts, and one species has even adapted to saltwater living.

Some iguanas like to live in groups, and it is not uncommon to see groups of 40 to 50 sunning themselves.

▲ These green, ring-tailed iguanas have found a rock to rest on in the South American forest.

◀ The rhinoceros iguana, with tiny horns on its snout, looks like a fierce mini-dinosaur. In captivity, however, it is peaceful and friendly.

◀ Gila Monster
The poisonous gila monster is too slow to chase down its dinner, so it feeds on eggs and new-born baby animals. Extra food is stored as fat in its thick tail, so a gila can live for more than a year without eating.

Frilled Lizard
The Australian frilled lizard spends most of its life in trees. However, if cornered on the ground, it rears on its back legs, extends the enormous frill around its head, opens its mouth wide, and *hissss-es* away.

Diving Iguanas
The marine iguana of the Galapagos Islands, 600 miles off the coast of South America, is the only lizard that has adapted to saltwater living. It can dive as deep as 30 feet to find the seaweed it likes to eat. After it leaves the cold water, the iguana climbs back on the rocks to bask in the hot sun.

Plumed Basilisk

Walking On Water
The basilisk of Central and South America can actually run on water! Taking advantage of its extra-long back feet and super speed, this lizard can go several strides before its lightweight body sinks in.

Plumed basilisks have sail-like crests that extend the full length of their bodies.

"Gek-oh, Gek-oh"
Chirping that sound is how the gecko got its name. These fascinating lizards are welcome visitors in many Asian homes. In addition to gobbling gobs of insects, some consider them a sign of good luck.

Geckos are wonderful climbers. The soft pads of the underside of their feet are equipped wth tiny, brush-like hooks. The hooks enable them to hang upside down on ceilings and cling to glass.

Some geckos can fly, too! By spreading an extra flap of skin along its body, the tiny flying gecko glides across the ▶ jungle treetops of Asia.

▼ West Indian Spotted Gecko

One Of A Kind ▲
Once mistaken for a lizard, the tuatara is the only remaining member of an entire group of ancient reptiles. The Maori people of New Zealand gave the tuatara its name, which means "peaks on the back."

Life begins slowly for the tuatara. An egg takes from twelve to fifteen months to hatch—longer than any other reptile. Life is long, though, usually lasting over 100 years.

The tuatara spends the hottest part of the day in its burrow, which it shares with sea birds. At night, it emerges to hunt. More so than other reptiles, the tuatara can remain active at very cold temperatures.

Spiked Defense ▼

Horned toads are small lizards with toadlike faces. Their bodies are covered with pointed spines and large "horns" which are extremely sharp. When frightened, a horned toad will sometimes squirt little streams of blood from the corners of its eyes.

Horned Toad

◀ Giant Lizard

Weighing as much as 350 pounds, the fierce Komodo dragon is the largest living lizard. It preys on large animals such as deer and wild boar, and has been known to attack and kill humans. When feeding, this lizard's jaws work so hard that it needs four new sets of teeth each year. Komodo dragons are only found on a few small Indonesian islands.

One of the tuatara's most interesting features is the third "eye," located on the top of its brain. Although skin covers the eye, it remains sensitive to light, but is unable to "see" images like a true eye.

TORTOISES AND TURTLES

Giant Tortoise

About 250 species of turtles and tortoises—the only reptiles with shells—inhabit the warmer areas of the Earth. The turtle's shell system has protected it so well that turtles have lived on Earth, practically unchanged, for about 200 million years.

Diamondback Terrapin

When this painted turtle feels threatened, it tucks itself into its "home" until the danger passes. ▼

Green Sea Turtle

What's in a name?
The name turtle usually refers to animals that live in freshwater—lakes, rivers, ponds, and streams. Sea turtles live in the ocean. Turtles that spend most or all of their time on land are called tortoises. Terrapin, a native American word meaning "little turtle," refers to small freshwater turtles, in particular the diamondback terrapin.

— Carapace

— Plastron

Scute Pattern

◀ Either a layer of tough leathery skin, or hard plates called scutes [scoots] cover the shell. Each species has its own scute pattern which keeps getting larger as the turtle grows.

Shell System
The turtle's shell is part of its skeleton. The shell is made up of two parts, the curved upper part (carapace) and the flattish lower part (plastron).

Clever and Deadly

Although toothless, this American snapping turtle is ready to use its strong, sharp beak to deliver a vicious bite. The snapper prefers to live in quiet muddy streams and ponds where it can snap away at fish, frogs, and water birds.

The alligator snapping turtle lies camouflaged in the mud with its mouth open. The turtle wriggles a worm-like pink flap on its tongue to lure small fish inside its deadly jaws.

Instead of teeth, turtles have beak-like jaws which snap and chop plants and small animals into bite-sized pieces. On land, turtles feed mainly on slow-moving prey, such as insects and worms. Many eat plants, too. Tortoises are vegetarians.

Loose fringes of skin dangle from the neck and head of the South American matamata turtle. Mistaking the fringes for worms, fish are lured close to its jaws. Suddenly, the strange-looking matamata opens wide and sucks in its dinner!

◀ **Soft Shell**
Turtles that spend most of their lives in freshwater tend to have lighter, flatter shells than land turtles. Instead of hard, horny plates, the streamlined body of this spiny soft-shelled turtle is covered by leathery skin.

Boxed In
The eastern box turtle lives in damp fields and forests. When threatened, a hinge on its plastron (underside) allows it to tuck itself tightly into its protective shell.

Long Distance Travelers
▲ Some green sea turtles migrate over 2,000 miles across the Atlantic Ocean to lay their eggs on the same beach on which they were born. Weighing less than an ounce, these babies all hatch together and quickly dash to the safety of the sea.

A swimming sea turtle is the world's fastest reptile. Its lightweight, streamlined shell and strong, flat flippers help propel the sea turtle through the ocean at speeds up to 20 mph.

◀ **Old Timers**
Galapagos tortoises can grow up to four feet in shell length and weigh as much as 600 pounds. These land giants have strong thick legs to support their weight. Tortoises live longer than any other animal—some have lived more than 150 years!

Basking Together ▶
A group of painted turtles bask under the warm sun. Like all reptiles, cold-blooded turtles need the sun's warmth to raise their blood temperature. Painted turtles, the most numerous small turtles in North America, like to bask in groups.

Turtle Tears ▶

This tearful loggerhead sea turtle isn't sad because she's leaving over 100 of her eggs on shore. She may have gotten sand in her eyes when she covered her nest, or she's simply "crying" away the extra salt she swallowed swimming in the salty ocean.

Green Sea Turtle

Giant

The leatherback sea turtle is by far the largest of all turtles—on land or in the sea. Weighing up to 1,500 pounds, this giant can dive almost three-quarters of a mile before coming up for air. Instead of a hard, rigid shell, the leatherback is covered with tough, leathery skin.

Leatherback Turtle

▲This mother-to-be is laying her eggs into a recently dug nest. All turtles, even those who live in the sea, lay eggs on land—although never far from water. Turtles do not take care of their eggs or babies. The sun's warmth or heat created by rotting vegetation keeps the eggs warm until they hatch.

A newly hatched eastern box turtle.

AMPHIBIANS

This leopard frog, a common species in North America, catches a dragonfly with its sticky tongue.

Frogs, toads, salamanders, and caecilians—these creatures of both land and water make up the vertebrate group known as amphibians. Like reptiles, amphibians are cold-blooded— their body temperature varies with their surroundings. But they are not covered with scales. They actually breathe air through their skin, as well as through lungs.

LET'S EAT
Most amphibians are meat-eaters and will gulp down almost any live food they can swallow. Spiders, insects, earthworms, and slugs are common meals. The bigger amphibians, such as the bullfrog, may even eat mice, birds, and small snakes.

SIZING UP AMPHIBIANS
Resembling giant worms, caecilians are limbless and blind, and grow as long as five feet. The giant salamander may grow to over five feet long. The Goliath frog can be three feet long and weigh seven pounds. Only about half an inch long, the Cuban pygmy frog may be the smallest amphibian.

▲ A Giant Salamander

◀ Red-eyed tree frogs

SO MANY FROGS
Of the more than 4,000 known amphibian species, frogs and toads account for about 3,800. Some frogs are completely aquatic and have fully webbed toes. Some live under ground, in burrows. Others live in trees and have suction cups at the end of their fingers and toes for holding on to leaves and branches.

EGGS IN THE WATER

Unlike reptile eggs, amphibian eggs do not have a shell for protection. Amphibians must lay their eggs in the water to keep them from drying out. Some lay thousands of eggs, leaving them to hatch and grow. Others take better care of their eggs. The pygmy marsupial frog (right) keeps her eggs under her skin until they hatch.

▲ This colorful tadpole will develop into a tree frog.

◀ Costa Rican rain frogs develop fully in their egg, never passing through a tadpole stage.

CHANGING SHAPES

Most amphibians spend the first part of their life in water before moving onto land. After hatching from their egg, amphibians go through a larval stage. We call frogs and toads at this in-between stage *tadpoles*. It usually takes about 12 to 16 weeks for a newly hatched tadpole to change into a completely formed frog or toad.

The mud puppy, actually a kind of salamander, keeps its feathery larval gills even as an adult.

▲ The arrow-poison frog carries its young to a nearby pool when the tadpoles are grown and ready to swim.

KILLER COLORS

Their bright colors warn predators to back off, because arrow-poison frogs pack a deadly poison. There are about 40 known species, and none is longer than 2 inches. Found in the rain forests of Central and South America, the frogs are useful to native peoples, who coat darts with the poison then hunt jaguars and monkeys.

Photo Credits: Birds of Prey

Robert E. Barber: pages 90, 91, 105
Bill Beatty: page 90
W. Perry Conway: pages 84, 88, 90, 91, 92-93, 96, 100, 104
Dwight Kuhn: page 100
Tom & Pat Leeson: pages 82, 103
Frank Oberle: page 105
A. B. Sheldon: page 100
Lynn M. Stone: pages 82, 85, 99, 103
Tom Bledsoe/DRK: pages 88, 97
John Cancalosi/DRK: pages 87, 99
Marty Cordano/DRK: page 105
Gerard Fuehrer/DRK: pages 94-95
Lisa Husar/DRK: pages 87, 97
M. P. Kahl/DRK: pages 83, 95, 98, 102
Steve Kaufman/DRK: pages 84, 87, 88, 96, 101
Stephen J. Krasemann/DRK: page 86
Wayne Lankinen/DRK: page 95
Tom & Pat Leeson/DRK: pages 86-87
Wayne Lynch/DRK: page 84
S. Nielsen/DRK: pages 84-85
Leonard Lee Rue, III/DRK: pages 86, 96
George J. Sanker/DRK: page 83
John Winnie, Jr./DRK: page 85
Jeremy Woodhouse/DRK: page 93
Belinda Wright/DRK: pages 89, 98
Bill Banaszewski/Visuals Unlimited: page 104
Gerard & Buff Corsi/Visuals Unlimited: page 102
Beth Davidow/Visuals Unlimited: page 97
Gil Lopez-Espina/Visuals Unlimited: page 103
Ken Lucas/Visuals Unlimited: pages 83, 88
Barbara Magnuson/Visuals Unlimited: page 89
Maslowski/Visuals Unlimited: pages 82, 101
Joe McDonald/Visuals Unlimited: page 94
A. & E. Morris/Visuals Unlimited: pages 104-105
Fritz Polking/Visuals Unlimited: pages 86, 99
Tom J. Ulrich/Visuals Unlimited: page 94
Robert Franz/Wildlife Collection: page 98
Martin Harvey/Wildlife Collection: pages 82, 87, 92, 102-103
Henry Holdsworth/Wildlife Collection: pages 101, 105
HPH Photography/Wildlife Collection: page 99
Charles Melton/Wildlife Collection: page 89
Tom Vezo/Wildlife Collection: page 100

Birds of Prey

BIRDS THAT PREY

Birds of prey are meat-eating birds that use their strong feet to catch and kill prey. They also have strong, hooked beaks for tearing into flesh. Birds of prey are sometimes called raptors.

The bald eagle.

SHE'S BIGGER
Unusual among birds, raptor females are generally bigger than males. In some species, such as the little sparrowhawk (left), the female may be twice as big. Other raptors show less difference. Among species of vultures, males and females are about the same size.

▶ DAY AND NIGHT
Most birds of prey are diurnal—active during the day. Most owls, however, are nocturnal. They do their hunting at night, relying on their hearing and low-light vision to locate prey.

SIMPLY BIRDS
Many birds, like the heron at right, eat other animals. But they are not called birds of prey, because they do not have the same kind of body or hunting methods that eagles, hawks, and other birds of prey do.

BIG AND ▲ LITTLE

Raptors come in all sizes. Biggest of them all, the Andean condor (above) may weigh 25 pounds and have wings stretching to over 10 feet. It's about 250 times heavier than the smallest bird of prey, the tiny Asian falconet.

TOP OF THE HEAP

Raptors, such as this martial eagle, sit at the top of the food chain. Much like a lion, they hunt other animals, but almost nothing else hunts them. Their only enemies are other birds of prey and humans.

WEAK FEET

Vultures, such as this white-backed vulture, are considered birds of prey even though their feet are weak. Because vultures feed mainly on carrion (dead animals), lacking grasping power is not a big problem for them. Their beaks do all the work!

A HUNTER'S BODY

Birds of prey have a body suited for hunting other animals. From beak to tail feathers, every part serves a purpose.

A peregrine falcon.

▼FINE FEATHERS
Feathers do many jobs for birds of prey. Soft down keeps the birds warm. Strong feathers on the wings allow the birds to control flight. Tail feathers are used for steering and braking. The flight feathers on the wings of many owls, including this great horned owl, have a soft edge that makes flight noiseless.

TALONS OF DOOM▼
If you were a bird of prey, your toenails would be talons. A raptor's talon-tipped feet are its most important weapon. Some fish-eating raptors, such as this osprey, have specially curved claws and spiny bumps on their feet to help them hook and hang on to their wriggling catch.

▲NO CHEWING
Raptors, such as this Steller's sea eagle, have a big, strong beak that is great for tearing meat. But they don't have heavy teeth and jaws for chewing, because that would weigh them down. They do their chewing inside a part of the stomach called the gizzard. The gizzard's strong muscles contract around the food, grinding it against the rough inner surface to break it down.

WONDER WINGS ▼

Raptors that spend lots of time soaring have long, broad wings. By catching rising air currents, a bird like the turkey vulture (below) can cruise for hours and barely flap its wings. Soaring saves a lot of energy. Falcons, on the other hand, are fast-flapping flyers. Their narrow, pointed wings enable them to maneuver easily.

LIGHT BONES

To be able to fly well, birds of prey must weigh as little as possible. Hollow, air-filled bones are light but strong. Raptor skeletons are so light that in some species, such as the bald eagle, the bird's feathers weigh more than its bones!

EYE MOVEMENT

Raptor eyes are so big that they cannot move in their socket. The bird has to turn its whole head to look around. Raptors rely on their eyes and must avoid injuring them. A bony ridge above the eye gives some protection. Raptors also have a tough, partly transparent third eyelid that closes over their eyes to protect them when the birds are attacking prey or flying through branches.

EAGLE EYES

Birds of prey have eyesight that is at least two to three times better than ours. Some can see a grasshopper from a hundred yards away—the length of a football field! Eagles, such as the golden eagle (right), can spy rabbits and other prey from over a mile away.

GRABBING A MEAL

The ways raptors hunt are as varied as the foods they eat. Most hunt from the sky, but on occasion some will chase rabbits on foot through thick underbrush. The four-foot-tall secretary bird (below) prefers hunting on the ground. It walks in the grass of the African savannas looking for snakes. When it finds one, the secretary bird stomps on the snake to kill it.

TAKING THE PLUNGE ▲
The osprey is one of the few raptors to use this hunting technique: Soaring hundreds of feet above the water, looking for fish, it will tuck its wings in and dive as soon as it spots some prey. Just before hitting the water, it throws its wings back and plunges in feet first. Then it flaps out of the water with its catch.

◄ TEAMWORK
Most raptors hunt alone, but some hunt in pairs. Red-tailed hawks team up to capture gray squirrels. The one at left has caught a rat! However, only Harris's hawks hunt in family groups the way wolves do. As many as six may work in relays to chase prey.

PIRATE RAPTORS
Some raptors, including the African fish eagle (left), are aerial pirates. They annoy other birds carrying food, until the food is dropped. Then the pirate bird either catches the food in mid-air or picks it up from the ground. African fish eagles rob ospreys, herons, and even each other.

WHERE THERE'S FIRE
For many birds of prey, wildfires mean food. The birds gather to catch insects and other animals fleeing from the flames. Flocks of fifty to a hundred crested caracaras have been spotted feeding near the edge of grass fires.

▼ SWEET LARVAE
Honey-buzzards go searching for bee and wasp nests. They dig the nests out of the ground, and eat the insects and honey. Their favorite bits seem to be the larvae—newly hatched, immature insects—which the honey-buzzards pick up one by one. Short, stiff feathers help protect the birds from being stung on the face.

▲ LOW & SLOW
Raptors often cruise back and forth close to the ground searching for their next meal. They look for movement and listen for the tiny sounds made by a scurrying mouse, vole, or other prey.

SIT & WAIT ▲
The most common way that birds of prey hunt is to sit and wait for something to happen. This Harris's hawk has chosen a perch that gives it a good view. It will watch very carefully for prey, then quickly swoop down to make its catch.

HOME, SWEET HOME

Birds of prey live on every continent except Antarctica. They may hunt over rain forest, desert, mountain, or prairie. Some raptors make long migrations each spring and fall, following food supplies and warm weather.

A Steller's sea eagle in Japan scans the water for prey.

IN THE RAIN FOREST

A chunk of South American rain forest may be home to more than fifteen raptor species, including large birds of prey, such as the harpy eagle (right). The lush and varied food supply makes the rain forest an ideal habitat. The harpy eagle hunts sloths, monkeys, and other animals that make their home in the treetops.

These red-tailed hawks have made their nest in a saguaro cactus in Arizona.

HOT AIR

Migrating birds, such as the turkey vulture (above), avoid crossing large bodies of water. Thermals—columns of warm, rising air on which these birds soar—do not form over water. Raptors save energy on long flights by letting a thermal carry them up like an elevator. Then they glide "downhill" until they catch the next thermal.

LONG TRIP

Hundreds of thousands of Swainson's hawks migrate each year. A Swainson's hawk traveling from Montana to its winter home in Argentina may fly over 6,000 miles each fall. In the spring, it flies the same distance on the flight back. The trip can take up to two months each way. Biologists are not quite sure, but they think that these birds do not eat at all while migrating.

MILLIONS OVERHEAD

Millions of migrating raptors riding thermals are brought together where the land narrows between two bodies of water. More than any other place, Veracruz, Mexico, sees the greatest number of migratory birds each year. Almost a million hawks might go by in a single day. In the fall of 1995, watchers counted 20 species and more than 4 million birds.

BIG RANGE

Many raptor species are found in only a relatively small area, in some cases on a single island. The black-shouldered kite (right) is found in very limited ranges in Europe and North America. Ospreys and peregrine falcons, on the other hand, are adaptable enough to live almost anywhere in the world.

MAKING A NEST

Raising a family is a big part of a raptor's life. Some species, such as bald eagles (left), may use the same nest for generations, adding to it each year. One nest was found to measure 10 feet wide and 20 feet deep, and weighed nearly 2 tons! In many species, the female decides the location for a new nest, and often does the building. The male brings in construction materials.

A fuzzy, day-old eastern screech owl waits for its nest mates to hatch.

MATES

Many raptor mates stay together for a number of breeding seasons. When making courtship flights, some fly in big swoops as high up as 1,000 feet, then dive down. Others fly together as pairs, one above the other. The bird underneath rolls over in mid-flight to touch talons with the bird above. Bald eagles grab each other's talons and cartwheel downward.

A LOT OF EGGS

Most diurnal birds of prey lay one to six eggs, depending on the species. Snowy owls sometimes lay a dozen! But raptors don't lay all their eggs at once. They wait a day or two after each egg before laying the next. The first chick to hatch is bigger than the others, and may kill its nest mates, especially if food is scarce. By eliminating competition, the chick ensures its survival.

Ferruginous hawks make their nest in the grasslands of the western U.S., where they may lay two to six eggs.

Just weeks after hatching, raptors begin to molt, growing their juvenile feathers. This four-week-old golden eagle, still partially downy, attempts a defensive posture.

AIRBORNE

The period of time lasting from the day a chick hatches from its egg to the day it takes its first flight is called the fledgling period. It may be as short as 23 days for small birds of prey, and as long as 130 days for large eagles. Condors have the longest fledgling period—up to 150 days.

▲ This young bald eagle is exercising its wings.

GO, DAD! ▶
From just before the eggs are laid until about midway through the nesting period, most male raptors are very busy providing food. Once males bring the food to the nest, it is up to the females to tear off pieces for the chicks.

FALCONS

Fast, fast, fast—that's the best way to describe falcons. With their long, pointed wings, they can really zip! Some specialize in catching birds.

FAST & DEADLY ▶

The peregrine does its hunting in the air, swooping or diving down onto its prey with incredible speed—nearly 200 miles per hour—and delivering a killing blow with the hind talon protruding from its closed feet. Normally cliff-nesting birds, peregrine falcons have adapted to nesting in cities. Large populations of rock doves (pigeons) keep them well fed.

BIG & LITTLE ▶

Two feet tall with a five-foot wingspan, the gyrfalcon (right) is the largest and probably fastest falcon. It often captures prey by surprise, either "binding to it" (grabbing it in mid-air) or stunning it and returning to catch the prey as it falls. The smallest falcon, the sparrow-sized black-thighed falconet, is also the smallest of all raptors.

◀ **DANGEROUS MEETINGS**

Even among falcons, it is a rare feat to capture and kill a bird flying in the opposite direction. Only the lanner falcon (left) displays the coordination and timing needed to pull off a "head-on" kill.

▼YUM, ROADKILL
Not as speedy as their falcon relatives, caracaras do most of their hunting on the ground, scavenging for whatever they can find. Often described as clever birds, caracaras may steal food from campers. Others have learned to cruise the highways at dawn to find whatever may have been hit and killed by cars during the night.

HOVERCRAFT
Falcons known as kestrels hunt by kiting, or hovering, over one spot. They do this by flying very slowly into the wind, balancing their speed with the wind's. When they spot prey, they dive hundreds of feet to make the kill.

◀ The robin-sized American kestrel is one of the smallest falcons.

PLAN AHEAD
Many falcons cache, or store, extra food, which gives them something to fall back on if prey is scarce. They stash food in a variety of places, including hollow trees, rain gutters, and switchboxes on utility poles.

KITES & HARRIERS

Although they're not very fast fliers, kites are graceful in the air. Harriers, like the one below, hunt by flying slowly close to the ground. Because their feet and legs are weaker than those of other hawks, kites and harriers hunt small mammals, frogs, snakes, and insects.

◀ The Brahminy kite, which ranges from India to Australia, preys on frogs, crabs, fish, and insects.

SNAIL ▶ SNACKS

Florida's snail kite is a snail specialist, eating no other prey. Its long, curved bill allows it to pull the snail from its shell. A snail kite's feeding perch can be identified by the pile of empty shells that lies beneath it.

LISTEN, LISTEN

The northern harrier is the only day-flying bird of prey in North America with sound-focusing facial discs. These discs, formed by feathers arranged like a shallow bowl, capture the slightest sounds. The harrier can find vole nests hidden in tall grasses by listening for the rodents' squeaks.

MID-AIR MEALS ▼
The swallow-tailed kite doesn't wait to land before eating its food. All prey, including insects, snakes, and lizards, are consumed in mid-air. This kite has even been observed snatching up a whole nest and then, while still in flight, eating the young birds within, one by one.

LUNCH PASS
When a male harrier has food to give to his mate and their chicks, he doesn't always just take it to the nest. Sometimes he calls the female to fly out and meet him. Then he flies above her and drops the food. She catches it in her talons and takes it back to the nest while the male resumes hunting.

▲ LOW LIFE
Harriers often make their nests on the ground, hidden among tall grasses or reeds. After she builds the nest, the female lays her eggs. She usually lays only three or four, but if there's plenty of food around she may lay as many as ten.

BIRDS OF A FEATHER ▲
Birds of prey most often fly together when they migrate. Small raptors, such as kites, form flocks to gain information about where to find insects and other small prey.

HAWKS & BUZZARDS

Because of their short, rounded wings, most hawks are quick and able to maneuver through wooded areas when chasing prey. Buzzards are quite similar to hawks, and are sometimes called hawks, especially in North America. Buzzards tend to have longer, wider wings and shorter tails than hawks, and they are better suited for open country.

▼ The black-collared hawk, found in Central and South America, preys on fish, grasping its catch with feet specially equipped with spines.

◀ **WILD EYES**
When they are small chicks, Cooper's hawks have gray eyes. By the time they are a year old, their eye color has changed to a bright yellow. From then on, their eyes will gradually darken, becoming orange, then finally red.

DEADLY & DETERMINED
The goshawk dives into thick brush and scrambles over branches in pursuit of prey. It can weave through the forest at high speed, and often takes squirrels, rabbits, and birds by surprise.

CONFUSED? ▶
The most common buzzard in North America is called the red-tailed hawk. If that's not confusing enough for you, red-tails often fill in for eagles on TV and in the movies. The red-tailed hawk's screaming call is used in place of the bald eagle's creaky cackle.

◀ IN BETWEEN
Harris's hawk has a hawklike shape but buzzardlike behavior. This unusual raptor likes to use the top of a giant saguaro cactus as a hunting perch, and it often builds its nest in the saguaro's branches.

NO PERCH NEEDED ▲
The ferruginous hawk, actually a buzzard, prefers to hunt in open areas. It may hover while hunting ground squirrels and rabbits. Or it may just land and hunt from the ground, even if perches such as fence posts and telephone poles are nearby.

EAGLES

There are about 60 species of eagles living around the world. The smallest, the Nias serpent-eagle, has a wingspan of about three feet. The huge harpy eagle has a wingspan of about eight feet and weighs nearly 20 pounds—almost twice as much as a bald eagle.

SALMON FEAST ▼
Although eagles are usually solitary, big food supplies can draw a crowd. Between October and December, as many as 3,000 eagles may gather in the trees along the Chilkat River in Alaska. The eagles feed on dead and dying salmon that have spawned in the river.

A cat snake is easy prey for the crested serpent-eagle.

SNAKE SNACKS ▲
Snake-eagles and serpent-eagles prey on snakes almost exclusively. The short-toed snake-eagle often swallows its catch whole, leaving just the tail hanging out. If the eagle has a hungry chick to feed, it returns to the nest. The youngster grabs the tail and pulls, neatly retrieving the snake from the adult.

BIG & STRONG
Africa's biggest eagle, the martial eagle (left), has a wingspan of about eight feet and may weigh as much as 13 pounds. It can kill small antelopes and jackals. Quite a bit smaller, the crowned hawk-eagle takes similar-sized prey and is known as Africa's most powerful eagle.

◀ FRUIT, PLEASE
The rather weird palm-nut vulture looks like a cross between a vulture and an eagle. Its diet is also unusual, because it prefers palm fruit to meat, eating other food, such as crabs and shellfish, only occasionally.

DIVING DEEP ▲
Ospreys are not eagles but have life-styles similar to some of the fish-eating eagles. Like these eagles, ospreys regularly pluck fish from near the water's surface. But ospreys are the only ones that will dive deep to pursue their finny prey.

The huge harpy eagle is considered to be the world's most powerful bird.

CRUISING ▶
Many eagles fly only about four to six hours each day. But the colorful bateleur takes to the skies early, gliding with its long, narrow wings for most of the day. Cruising over African plains at 35 to 50 miles per hour, it often covers 300 miles in a day.

OWLS

When the day-hunting raptors roost for the night, owls begin their hunt. On silent wings, they fly out in search of prey, using specialized senses—acute hearing and good night vision.

▲ A saw-whet owl catches a mouse.

FACE THE LIGHT▼
Most owls prefer to hunt in low light, either at dawn and dusk or throughout the night. But when owls have chicks to feed, they may hunt during the day as well. For some owls, such as the snowy owl (below), there is no choice. During the summer, snowy owls nesting in the Arctic have no nights in which to hunt!

BURROWING OWLS▲
Unlike most other owls, these unusual owls run well on the ground, form social groups, and live in burrows abandoned by ground squirrels or prairie dogs. When frightened, baby burrowing owls buzz like rattlesnakes, imitating these reptiles that also live in old burrows.

▲BIG & SMALL
Owls can be found on every continent except Antarctica. The largest is Europe's eagle owl (above), weighing in at six and a half pounds. The smallest, standing only about six inches tall, is the elf owl, found in the southwestern United States. It weighs slightly less than a golf ball.

◀ **FISHY STORY**
When fishing owls spot a fish near the water's surface, they swoop down to scoop it up, using long curved talons. Unlike other owls, fishing owls have featherless feet and legs—feathers would get too wet and messy.

FOOD FACTS
Unlike other raptors, owls do not eat carrion. Most owls prey on rodents. Smaller owls, such as the screech owl (right), feed on insects.

▲ **BE VERY QUIET**
The great gray owl will sometimes plunge into a smooth stretch of snow and come up with a mouse. Apparently, the owl can hear the rodents chewing in their tunnels beneath the surface. The barn owl and long-eared owl can hunt in complete darkness, using only their hearing to find prey.

101

VULTURES

As gruesome as they may seem, vultures play a very important role: They clean up. Without vultures, rotting carcasses would spread disease, not to mention stink up things! It is believed that vultures in Africa eat more meat than do all the other predators combined.

LET'S MEAT UP

Up to six kinds of vultures may gather at a large carcass in Africa. Large vultures, like the lappet-faced vulture (left), may be the only ones capable of ripping into the fresh carcass of a large animal, or eating tough parts such as bone and skin. Smaller vultures follow, eating the softer parts, sometimes climbing right inside a carcass to get at the meat.

◀ BALD IS BEAUTIFUL

It makes perfect sense that the king vulture has a bare head, because this carrion-eating bird sticks its head into gooey, rotting carcasses. After eating, most vultures enjoy a bath and will sometimes fly a great distance to find water.

LIKE A STORK?
Unlike their Old World relatives, vultures in the Americas, such as these black vultures, are more closely related to storks than to birds of prey. They have a keen sense of smell, while Old World vultures rely on sight and can locate food only in open country.

BONE DROP ▼
Bearded vultures, or lammergeiers, prefer to eat bones. Small bones are swallowed whole, but bigger ones pose a problem. So bearded vultures carry the bones into the sky, as high up as 200 feet, then drop them onto the rocks below, breaking them into edible bits. The vultures employ the same strategy with tortoises.

EGGS-ACTLY ▶
Egyptian vultures like to eat ostrich eggs, and they crack them open in a very interesting way. Small eggs are just picked up and thrown down. When eggs are too big to pick up, the vultures pick up stones and throw them until the eggs break—one of the few examples of tool use by an animal.

▼ SMELL THAT?
The turkey vulture has an exceptionally good sense of smell, and can find carrion hidden beneath the rainforest canopy. It can tell the difference between edible meat and stuff that has become too rotten even for a vulture.

PEOPLE & BIRDS OF PREY

At first we treated raptors with respect, telling stories about their magic powers. Then we began to hunt them, often for no reason at all. About 50 years ago, we started using a lot of chemicals on the land that caused raptors to have trouble laying eggs that would hatch. But then we began to value birds of prey, and we started working to help them survive.

This golden eagle takes an up-close look at some fascinating school children.

▲ FARMER'S FRIEND

Golden eagles, such as the one above, are a big help to ranchers. They prey on rabbits and ground squirrels, which eat a lot of grass meant for sheep and cattle. Grain farmers should be happy to see hawks, because hawks hunt mice that eat the grain.

HUNTING TOGETHER

The sport of falconry—using a trained bird of prey to hunt game—is probably about 4,000 years old. Today, many falconers are involved in raptor conservation. In the U.S., they are legally allowed to use some species of raptors from the wild. They also continue to breed many raptor species in captivity for use in falconry.

GOOD CHANGE

Hawk Mountain, Pennsylvania, sits on a major flyway for migrating birds of prey. Hunters used to go there to shoot hawks passing overhead. Now Hawk Mountain is a sanctuary where bird watchers gather to see the almost 20,000 raptors that pass through each fall.

POWERFUL PLUMES

Most North American Indians used bald eagle and golden eagle feathers for religious and ceremonial purposes. Today, when one of these protected birds of prey is found dead, a government agency may give the feathers to a group of Native Americans.

IN TROUBLE

Many of the most endangered birds of prey, such as northern spotted owls, are in trouble because their habitat is disappearing. Other raptors have been hunted or poisoned. The California condor (left), the largest raptor in North America, is one of the rarest animals on earth. Fewer than one hundred California condors are living today.

▼RAPTOR REHAB

Injured birds of prey are cared for at raptor centers around the world. Birds that can fly and hunt are released back into the wild. Those that are unable to catch prey are cared for in captivity, and are often used to educate people about birds of prey.

▼LENDING A HAND

Scientists sometimes raise raptor chicks to release into wild areas that would make good homes. Because scientists don't want the birds to associate humans with food, the caretakers feed the chicks using a hand puppet shaped like an adult eagle's head.

Index

African elephants, 9
African fish eagles, 87
African honeybees, 51
Alligators, 58, 59, 60, 61
Alligator snapping turtles, 75
American snapping turtles, 75
Amphibians, 78-79
Anacondas, 64-65
Anteaters, 18
Ants, 30, 31, 33, 36, 37, 41, 42, 46, 47
Apes, 8, 26
Aphids, 33
Army cutworm moths, 33
Arrow-poison frogs, 79
Asian falconets, 83
Australian blue-tongued skinks, 68
Australian frilled lizards, 71

Bald eagles, 82, 90, 91, 97, 105
Banded sphinx moths, 30
Barn owls, 101
Basilisks, 72
Bateleurs, 99
Bats, 8, 21
Bearded vultures, 103
Beavers, 17
Bees, 30, 32, 33, 36, 37, 43, 46, 48, 49, 51
Beetles, 30, 31, 32, 33, 34, 35, 37, 43, 44-45, 48, 50, 53
Black-collared hawks, 96
Black-footed ferrets, 27
Black-thighed falconets, 93
Black vultures, 103
Bluebottle flies, 43
Blue racer snakes, 62
Blue whales, 9
Boas, 62-63, 64
Bullfrogs, 78
Bumblebees, 33
Burrowing owls, 100
Butterflies, 30, 32, 34, 36, 38-39, 41, 51, 52
Buzzards, 87, 96-97

Caddis flies, 32
Caimans, 58
Camel crickets, 53
Camels, 15
Cape buffalo, 22
Capybaras, 17
Caracaras, 87, 93
Carrion beetles, 32
Caterpillars, 33, 36, 40, 41, 48, 51, 53
Chameleons, 56, 68-69
Cheetahs, 20

Chimpanzees, 8
Cobras, 67
Cockroaches, 36, 41, 51, 53
Colorado potato beetles, 50
Compass termites, 47
Condors, 83, 91, 105
Cooper's hawks, 96
Copperheads, 66
Coral snakes, 65, 67
Cougars, 20
Coypus, 12
Crested-serpent eagles, 98
Crickets, 43, 53
Crocodilians, 56, 57, 58-61
Crowned hawk-eagles, 98
Cuban pygmy frogs, 78

Deer mice, 15
Diamondback terrapins, 74
Dinosaurs, 8
Dolphins, 11, 16, 21
Double-headed lizards, 69
Dragonflies, 33, 36, 40, 43
Dung beetles, 44

Eagle owls, 100
Eagles, 82, 83, 85, 87, 88, 90, 91, 97, 98-99, 104, 105
Eastern box turtles, 76, 77
Eastern hognosed snakes, 63
Eastern screech owls, 90
Echidnas, 24
Egyptian vultures, 103
Elf owls, 100
Elks, 13
Elytra, 44
Emerald tree boa, 62-63
European skippers, 50

Falconry, 104
Falcons, 84, 85, 89, 92-93
Ferruginous hawks, 90, 97
Fireflies, 43
Fishing owls, 101
Fleas, 30
Flies, 30, 31, 32, 33, 35, 36, 40, 42, 43, 48
Frogs, 21, 78-79
Fruit flies, 48
Fur seals, 13

Gaboon vipers, 66
Galagos, 12
Galápagos tortoises, 76
Garter snakes, 62, 63

Geckos, 68, 70, 72
Gharials, 58, 60
Giant pangolins, 25
Giant salamanders, 78
Giant tortoises, 74
Gila monsters, 71
Giraffes, 25
Gnats, 33
Golden eagles, 85, 88, 90, 104, 105
Golden lion tamarins, 27
Goliath beetles, 45
Goliath frogs, 78
Gorillas, 26
Goshawks, 96
Grasshoppers, 36, 48
Great gray owls, 101
Great horned owl, 84
Green sea turtles, 74, 76-77
Grizzly bears, 19
Gyrfalcons, 92

Harpy eagles, 88, 99
Harriers, 94-95
Harris's hawks, 86, 87, 97
Hawks, 82, 86, 87, 88, 89, 90, 96-97, 104
Hercules beetles, 45
Herons, 82, 87
Hippopotamuses, 17
Hognosed snakes, 63, 65
Honeybees, 37, 46, 49, 51
Honey-buzzards, 87
Horned toads, 73
Hornets, 33, 46, 47
Humpback whales, 19

Iguanas, 70-71
Impalas, 14

Jaguars, 15
Japanese macaques, 10
Jewel beetles, 31

Kangaroos, 11
Katydids, 41, 42
Kestrels, 93
Killer whales, *see Orcas*
King cobras, 67
King snakes, 65
King vultures, 102
Kites, 89, 94-95
Koalas, 18
Komodo dragons, 73

Ladybugs, 33

Lanner falcons, 92
Lappet-faced vultures, 102
Leatherback sea turtles, 77
Lemurs, 8, 27
Leopard frogs, 78
Lions, 11, 22
Lizards, 56, 57, 65, 68-73
Llamas, 14
Loggerhead sea turtles, 77
Long-eared owls, 101
Long-horned beetles, 35
Luna moths, 43

Mambas, 67
Manatees, 17
Martial eagles, 83, 98
Matamata turtles, 75
Mayflies, 32, 40
Meerkats, 23
Mongooses, 21
Monkeys, 8, 13, 25, 27
Moose, *see Elks*
Mosquitoes, 33, 40, 49
Moths, 30, 32, 33, 36, 38-39, 41, 43, 48
Mud puppies, 79
Musk oxen, 23

Narwhals, 16
Nias-serpent eagles, 98
Northern harriers, 94
Northern spotted owls, 105

Opossums, 23
Orcas, 21
Ospreys, 84, 86, 87, 89, 99
Owls, 82, 84, 90, 100-101, 105

Painted turtles, 76-77
Palm civets, 18
Palm-nut vultures, 99
Peregrine falcons, 84, 89, 92
Pine beetles, 48
Pit vipers, 66-67
Platypuses, 24
Polar bears, 15
Porcupines, 22
Prairie dogs, 27
Praying mantises (mantids), 37, 40, 49
Primates, 8
Proboscis monkeys, 25
Pronghorn deer, 23
Pygmy marsupial frogs, 79
Pygmy shrew, 9
Pythons, 63, 64, 65

Raccoons, 15, 19
Rainbow wood-borer beetles, 31
Rain frogs, 79
Rats, 15
Rattlesnakes, 66
Red-eyed tree frogs, 78
Red foxes, 9
Red-tailed hawks, 86, 88, 97
Rhinoceroses, 27
Rhinoceros vipers, 66
Right whales, 26
River dolphins, 16
Rocky Mountain bighorn sheep, 13
Rodents, 8, 12

Saddleback sows, 10
Salamanders, 78, 79
Saltwater crocodiles, 59, 61
Saw-whet owls, 100
Screech owls, 90, 101
Seals, 13, 15, 21
Sea otters, 16
Sea snakes, 63, 67
Sea turtles, 57, 74, 76-77
Secretary birds, 86
Serpent-eagles, 98
Sheep moths, 38
Shinglebacks, 69
Short-toed snake-eagles, 98
Silkworms, 48
Skinks, 68, 69, 70
Skunks, 22
Snake-eagles, 98
Snowshoe hares, 22
Snowy owls, 90, 100
Sparrowhawks, 82
Spider monkeys, 13
Spiny soft-shelled turtles, 76
Squirrels, 8

Star-nosed moles, 14
Steller's sea eagles, 84, 88
Stone flies, 36
Swainson's hawks, 89

Tarsiers, 8
Tasmanian devils
Termites, 18, 25, 30, 33, 34, 37, 46, 47
Three-toed sloths, 12
Tiger beetles, 53
Tigers, 8, 12
Toads, 78
Tortoises, 56, 74, 75, 76
Tree boas, 62-63, 64
Tree kangaroo, 24
Tree shrews, 8
Tuatara, 56, 57, 72-73
Turkey vultures, 85, 89, 103
Turtles, 56, 57, 74-77

Vine snakes, 65
Vipers, 63, 66-67
Vultures, 82, 85, 89, 99, 102-103

Walkingsticks, 41
Walruses, 10
Wasps, 33, 36, 37, 43, 46, 47, 53
Water bugs, 32
Water shrews, 21
Water striders, 41
Weevils, 45, 50
Wildebeests, 14
Wolves, 20
Worm lizards, 69

Yellow eyelash vipers, 66

Zebras, 14

Glossary

Amphibian: A cold-blooded vertebrate, such as a frog, toad, or salamander.
Antennae: Segmented sense organs, attached to an insect's head, that help it smell and touch.
Bird of prey: Meat-eating bird that uses its strong feet, talons, and hooked beak to catch and kill prey; also known as a raptor.
Camouflage: The way an animal disguises and protects itself by blending with its surroundings.
Carapace: The curved upper part of a turtle's shell.
Carnivore: An animal that eats the flesh of other animals.
Chrysalis: The hardened shell that a caterpillar creates around itself as it attaches itself to a tree limb or other structure and begins the process of metamorphosis into a butterfly.
Cocoon: The protective covering spun by the larva of an insect before it undergoes metamorphosis into its adult form.
Cold-blooded: Having a body temperature that is not regulated internally but adapts to the temperature of surrounding air or water.
Defoliator: An insect, such as certain caterpillars, that eats a tree's leaves but not its bark or wood.
Diurnal: Active during the day. Most raptors are diurnal hunters.
Egg tooth: A hard, sharp tooth on the beak or nose of unhatched birds and reptiles used to break out of the egg.
Elytra: The hard front wings of a beetle. The elytra fold tightly over the other set of wings like a cover.
Endangered: Threatened with extinction.
Entomologist: Scientist who studies insects.
Exoskeleton: A hard, outer skeleton or shell that protects an insect's fragile internal organs.
Extinction: The death of a population of animals caused by loss of habitat, predators, or the inability to adapt to changes in the environment.
Facets: The hundreds of eyes contained in the compound eyes of an insect.
Fossil: The remains or impression of an animal or plant naturally preserved in rock or other hard substances.
Fungus: Any member of the group of organisms called fungi, such as mold, rust, and mushrooms.
Gizzard: Part of a bird's stomach that contracts around unchewed food, breaks it down, and digests it.
Habitat: The place where an animal or plant naturally lives and grows.
Hemolymph: The blood of insects and other invertebrates.
Incubate: To keep eggs warm in order to hatch them.
Invertebrates: Animals that do not have backbones, such as insects, spiders, and earthworms.
Keratin: A protein that forms the basis of human skin, hair, and nails, as well as of horns, antlers, and lizard scales.
Kiting: Soaring or rising rapidly through the air.
Larva: A hatchling insect that does not look like its parents.
Mammal: A group of warm-blooded vertebrates that have hair and nourish their young with milk. Humans are mammals.
Metamorphosis: The changes in form during the life of an animal.
Migration: An animal's move away from or to its breeding or feeding grounds at certain times of the year.
Mimicry: The resemblance of a living creature to some other thing—such as a branch, flower, rock, or other animal—so as to deceive prey or predators.
Molt: To shed skin, feathers, hair, or a shell.
Nectar: Sweet liquid of certain plants; used to make honey.
Nocturnal: Active at night.
Nymph: A young insect that becomes adult through incomplete metamorphosis, molting many times until it resembles its parents.
Pits: Heat-sensing holes on either side of the nostrils of certain snakes that help locate warm-blooded prey.
Poacher: A person who kills or takes wild animals illegally.
Pollination: The process of fertilizing a plant by spreading pollen from flower to flower.
Predator: An animal that hunts other animals for food.
Prey: An animal that is hunted by other animals.
Primate: A group of mammals that can walk upright and use their hands to pick up things; this group includes humans, apes, monkeys, lemurs, and tarsiers.
Proboscis: The flexible, hollow tube that serves as a butterfly's mouth.
Pupa: The stage between larva and adult of a metamorphic insect, when legs, wings, and a new body are formed.
Reptile: A cold-blooded animal, usually covered with scales or bony plates, that slithers or crawls on its belly.
Rodent: A small mammal with sharp teeth, such as a mouse, squirrel, or rabbit.
Sanctuary: An area established for the protection of animals or natural resources.
Scavenger: An animal, such as a vulture, that feeds on dead rather than live animals.
Serrated: Having a notched edge, like on a saw.
Spawn: To produce eggs.
Species: A group of animals that produce offspring with each other but do not breed with other animals; an animal belonging to a biological classification.
Spiracle: A breathing hole along the outside of an insect's abdomen that allows air to flow inside the body.
Talon: The sharp, curving claw of a bird of prey.
Thermal: A rising body of warm air on which birds can soar.
Thorax: The middle of the three sections of an insect's body, where its wings and legs are located.
Trachea: Breathing tubes located in an insect's abdomen that make up its respiratory system.
Vegetarian: An animal that eats only vegetables and fruits; also known as a herbivore.
Venom: A poison that kills or injures. Some snakes and lizards have a venomous bite.
Warm-blooded: Having a fairly high and constant body temperature that is maintained internally, relatively independent of surroundings.
Wingspan: The distance from the tip of one wing to the tip of the other wing.